Bible-Based Counseling

Thanks Jeane;
and may this book
be a spirit Treasure
and Blessing to you.

may God show
Favor and grace
in your life.

Sincerely:
Mark Chapman, Jr.

Bible-Based Counseling

✦

A Professional Approach to Inner Healing and Personal Growth

Dr. Mark Chapman, Jr.

iUniverse, Inc.
New York Lincoln Shanghai

Bible-Based Counseling
A Professional Approach to Inner Healing and Personal Growth

iUniverse books may be ordered through booksellers or by contacting:

iUniverse
2021 Pine Lake Road, Suite 100
Lincoln, NE 68512
www.iuniverse.com
1-800-Authors (1-800-288-4677)

ISBN-13: 978-0-595-40101-7 (pbk)
ISBN-13: 978-0-595-84485-2 (ebk)
ISBN-10: 0-595-40101-5 (pbk)
ISBN-10: 0-595-84485-5 (ebk)

Printed in the United States of America

This book is dedicated to my:

Wife, Mildred, and Children: Margie, Mark III, Anita, Martin, Annette and Camilla, as well as our fourteen grandchildren, Father, and late Mother.

I commend my youngest Daughter, Camilla for her support and help in the development of this book. Your untiring effort from typing to proof reading the manuscript and developing the final layout and cover page, thank you Camilla.

Thank you Jason and Elizabeth (Granddaughter) for your help and support.

Contents

Introduction

I became interested in counseling while in the Navy, stationed on the Island of Diego Garcia located in the Indian Ocean. The first two groups I counseled were adults and adolescents. While engaged in Christian counseling, I also performed in-depth Premarital counseling dealing not only with the couple's compatibility but issues such as their finances, transportation, housing, etc. While serving as a Chaplain I was enabled by God, training and experience to help patients, and families go through grief, sorrow, pain, joy and comfort when their love one's were sick, preparing to go through surgery or had loss a family member, relative or friend.

I remember the first group counseling session I facilitated with eager third graders who were excited about the experience of being together and expecting great things. Before selecting two groups, I had two individual counseling sessions with each student to become acquainted and develop rapport. An individual counseling session had already been held with each parent or parents and I had an individual session with each parent once a month and one group session with all parents monthly.

These sessions were co-facilitated by the other Counselor who had fifteen children in her two groups. Interest in this new program was very high for parents, Counselors, and students. Parents found out that other parents in the group were experiencing many similar problems and concerns. The parents were able to solve many of their problems and we helped bring others to a successful resolution. In some cases problem-solving skills had to be taught. A battery of tests in reading, writing, math and social studies was completed as part of the selection process.

Their needs, strengths and weaknesses were already known but without developing a personal relationship the counseling session would not succeed. The children were chosen who were reading one, two, or three grade levels below their grade and had family problems or concerns. A Tutor was included in the program for remedial teaching where needed.

The method used to involve all students in the group session was to have them take turns reading a short story about a child or family situation. Then, facilitate the discussion and allow students to tell how it related to their life or situation at home, in school, or on the playground. There were eight students in one group and seven in the other. It was encouraging and very enlightening for their third grade teachers to see how these students blossomed and became more outgoing, able to express themselves in class to their teachers, other classmates in their group and non-group members. During individual counseling sessions held each week, students would use this time to talk about their family life and relationships with parents and siblings. They also talked about how they fit into their group.

By the end of the school year, some students advanced one, two, and a couple advanced three grade levels in their reading comprehension. Advances were also made in math, English, and Social Studies. The sheer joy I experienced seeing so much progress; children not wanting to miss neither their group nor their individual sessions is a testament to the effectiveness of this program. It was validated by pre. And post testing. Investing in our children is our number one priority.

When a student consults a guidance counselor for help in determining the student's aptitudes in terms of ability, the counselor examines the student's socio-economic background, tests indicating ability level, along with personal interests, family interests, and academic background.

These factors weigh heavily upon the counselor's advice to the student. A clear picture of the student's potential and ability can emerge when the major areas of his interests, ability, and academic records are analyzed. This is usually what the counselor will base his or her recommendations on and help the student to decide what career choices are best. However, many times a secular school will totally ignore the spiritual dimension of a student's life. In a Christian school this area would not be neglected.

Within the sphere of one's spiritual life swells the focus of hope, determination, and sense of wonder that enable many Christians to rise above their circumstances. I believe that God can help a person rise above his or her immediate situation. Many achievements have been accomplished because the person was committed and disciplined. This is not to say that ability is not important, but it does indicate that having focused direction, and a philosophy of life, add to whatever you already have.

1

The Third Force in Guidance Counseling

The Role of Self Worth in the Overall Development of the Student

Attitudes toward self slowly develop out of a myriad of what appears to be small, sometimes unnoticed developments within the family structure. John, the youngest of five children is allowed to get away with behavior that deserves some form of discipline. If he does not get his way when he is playing softball, he will sabotage the game.

As time passes, these unacceptable behaviors begin to shape how John feels about himself. He notices that more and more he is excluded from playing softball when teams are chosen. His sisters and brothers do not think his pranks are funny anymore. His mother and father are concerned.

John begins to feel unwanted by family and friends; he is having problems keeping up with his class in school. He feels his family has forgotten about him. Mother and father begin to realize they have not instilled values and discipline in John. After discussing their son's behavior with the school guidance counselor, and evaluating John's intelligence quotient test scores, test grades on schoolwork etc., both the counselor and his parents concluded that John had the ability to perform at a much higher academic level. His primary problem was that he had been mischievous, a prankster, who had become withdrawn and apathetic.

The guidance counselor worked out a method whereby parents and counselor would work together to help John feel better about himself. John's parents would meet with the other children and encourage them to be more affectionate and open with him. If he did something they felt offended by, they were to tell John this unacceptable behavior will not be tolerated. John's parents also agreed to talk to John about his behavior, express their love for him, and also inform John that

1

he would be disciplined for deviant conduct. As John continues to grow and mature, he has to develop a philosophy for life because: "There is no psychotherapy without a theory of man and a philosophy of life underlying it[1]."

With a channel of communication established among parents, children, and his counselor, John began to exhibit more self-worth. His grades improved, and he found new friends. John's guidance counselor was a valuable resource in helping solve a family problem.

I recall individual counseling sessions with Paul, a troubled kid that came from a broken home, did not have a father in his home and was rebellious toward his mother when she asked him to do daily chores. I was able to help Paul understand that even though he missed or felt cheated because he did not have a father to share time and experiences with, he should respect mom and be helpful by completing his assigned chores. I found a big brother for Paul who after a month started to show signs of improvement in his attitude and completed his chores without being told. Paul's grades improved, found more friends, and became more responsible. This was a real success story.

During adolescence, a person who is neither adult nor child is caught in the crosswinds of fast paced physical development that is hard for him to comprehend.

These statements brings focus because:

> In the course of maturing interests, the adolescent begins to evaluate the various facets of Western and American culture. As a result, views and concerns relating to education, religion, science and politics, emerge and grow as development advances. Strong cultural concerns are more closely related to early adulthood than to adolescence, but their appeal depends on the amount of stimulation in these fields the individual has received and his responsiveness to it.[2]

I can make one conclusion without reservation, that a struggling adolescent has much to comprehend, struggle with, and move on in a complex society. This is reason enough to hope that Christian guidance counselors can make their way into mainstream education. The writer does not see a problem with these counselors in Christian schools run by churches. In light of other religions outside the Christian faith, resistance toward placement of Christian counselors in the public school system would surface.

A solution to this problem is to cross-train Christian counselors in the basic doctrines of other religious faiths: Jewish, Moslem, Buddhist, etc.

The Role of Religion in Developing a Philosophy of Life

I believe that guidance counselors, teachers, and school administrators could perform their jobs better if students have been exposed to religious teaching and values. Even though a spiritual philosophy for life does not develop early in childhood, exposure to religious teachings, and values, tend to strengthen the child's inner self. Pikunas, Albrecht, and O'Neil state that:

> Religious maturation is often achieved at the college level, especially when education favors the development of a spiritual philosophy of life. Religion can be the basis for a very comprehensive and unifying philosophy since it identifies the goals and relationships of the individual during the present life and relates them to a life of happiness here-after as the chief goal for which to strive. For many adolescents then, religion can be the source of ideals and goals. When it's values and principles are clearly comprehended and accepted by an individual, it motivates and directs his behavior.[3]

Some of the finest schools in America have a religious orientation—Notre Dame, Texas Christian, etc. These schools turn out some of the brightest scholars. Many of these students have been in a religion-related school setting all their lives, and gain an extra edge over children trained in public schools because they have had the unifying force of God introduced into their lives at an early age. It is my observation over the past ten years that Children who attend church and Sunday school at an early age, tend to attend church more when they reach adolescence and adulthood. These influences have some bearing on what children and adolescents internalize during their formative years of physical, mental, moral, and spiritual development.

I believe that to the extent that a child or adolescent fails to develop in these areas, he or she will not fully develop an integrated, internal locus of control. A child has to be molded at an early age before the void is filled with inappropriate deviant behavior. Once a pattern of deviant conduct is developed, a child may use it as a means to attract attention to self, especially if he or she is a victim of parental neglect. The third force, God in his life, will make a difference.

I would like to make one point crystal clear. There are those who would point out that many lives have been ruined in the name of religion; and that religious cults exist in our society and in other lands which have beliefs counterproductive to good childhood discipline. Sometimes children are beaten, neglected, and taught doctrines that confuses and disorients. Not only children but adults have been brain washed by some false prophets' self styled religious philosophy. The Christian doctrine that I advocate is Bible-based under well-controlled circumstances with denominational approval.

The Effect of Curriculum and Teachers' Personalities on Students and Guidance Counseling

Guidance counselors bridge the gap between student and teacher. These are sensitive people, trained to deal with human conflict. When a child goes to school for the first time, it may be a terrifying experience. Usually parents will go with their children on the first day of school. For some children this is the first time they have ventured outside the protective environment of their family.

I know that an understanding teacher is a welcome sight to a child who may feel alone, lost, and confused in his or her new home away from home. Even at higher-grade levels and college, understanding teachers and professors help students adjust better to school. A cold, stern, demanding teacher can be a destructive or an interactive presence to a student striving to adjust to his or her new environment. A child, in these formative years, needs support, warmth, and caring to nurture personal and intellectual growth.

A teacher, who has Christ in his or her life, has something extra to share. Not that they would be witnessing, because young children are unable to grasp concepts of salvation, but the presence of God in the lives of teacher and counselor would manifest itself in how they relate to their students. The presence of God in the heart of the guidance counselor, when counseling or in helping others is the third force, the indwelling of the Holy Spirit mediating the thoughts and actions of the counselor. This teacher or counselor can deal with the teary-eyed youngster who may be feeling alone in the world on the first day of school.

Obtaining an education for our children is a national priority since:

> Education is a process in which the adolescent is deeply involved. Not only does it account for a major portion of his daily activity, it is also the sphere in which he experiences his rapidly expanding intellectual and social skills[4]

During this time of rapidly expanding and developing social and intellectual skills a key concern to the student is whether to go to college or enter skills training and go directly into the work force. A concerned guidance counselor is valuable to a student during this critical time in his or her life. I believe the student should consult with several people before making a decision. People usually know their own strengths, and weaknesses, without having them pointed out to them. In talking with several people, some will be honest, others will not. Talking with concerned family members and their pastor is helpful. The guidance counselor should be approached, probably more than once. You may not be compatible with your assigned counselor, and if this were true, you would need to seek the advice of another, because if personality becomes an obstacle, even if the counselor gives the student an honest assessment, he or she probably will not trust the advisor. Personalities do get in the way of progress at times. Since we cannot change people overnight, we have to move on. I have experienced a personality conflict with professors even though compatible with most people. The following statement is enlightening: "The curriculum, teachers' personalities; school-group relationships, and extra-curricular activities, are also factors affecting the student) directly.[5]"

The curriculum is most important whatever track the student takes because specific courses are required for college entrance or for special skills training. This is why it is important that the student receive the best advice possible about curriculum choices. I often think about the stress students endure trying to make decisions in the face of dealing with growth spurts, teachers' personalities, school-group relationships, extracurricular activities and personal problems.

The student may be a member of a church with a counseling staff. This could be a helpful resource in sorting out some of these problems related to dealing with life itself. Really sorting out routine problems dealing with school is part of growing up and the average adolescent should not experience much difficulty in dealing with them. The key is to know where to go for help. Overall, in the school setting, the teachers and counselors can help most. Guidance counselors are trained and have the expertise to advise the student on the correct and most appropriate curriculum.

Those guidance counselors who are equipped with additional help due to God's grace acting through their lives will be most helpful if they also have mastered their counseling skills and academics. Before any counselor can be helpful as a therapist, he or she must master the basic counseling techniques. A person cannot swim if he or she has not mastered the basic swimming strokes first. The person must know how to stay afloat, to kick properly to develop thrust, know how to tread water in case of an emergency, and must not fear water The same holds true for a counselor. Knowing and applying the basic counseling techniques is so essential that without mastering them the therapist will fail in his or her attempt to help the counseled.

Need for Cross-Culturally Trained Guidance Counselors

I see a need for cross-culturally trained counselors now more than at any other time, as more diverse culturally different people enter the United States each year. Though this country has many culturally different groups, many that come to this country have continued to maintain and nurture their own culture, language and mores. At times, counselor and counseled do not and cannot communicate in therapy because the counselor lacks the cross-cultural counseling knowledge and skills. Clients may not realize this is a barrier to the counseling process when selecting a counselor.

In November of 1988, I was blessed to sit under highly skilled and knowledgeable counselors, psychologists, and psychiatrists, at the "International Conference on Christian Counseling" which convened in Atlanta, Georgia. A broad range of Christian counseling perspectives, methodologies, and techniques were discussed. One was cross-cultural counseling. Dr. Hesselgrave writes concerning the importance of Christian counselors:

> The Christian counselor must be prepared to examine his theoretical understandings before he proceeds to diagnose the problems of the counseled and aid in their resolution. Only when he is faithful to God and His word in this twofold task, can his counseling be termed Christian.[6]

He further states that:

> Being a Christian in and of itself does not mean that the counselor's theory and practice are Christian. Then, to the extent that the Christian counselor actually directs the counseled to the right solutions to their problems and points the way to meaningful change, his counseling may also be termed effective.[7]

Cross-cultural Christian counseling needs attention, focus, and direction because it is sadly lacking in many areas of the U.S. This statement is overdue because:

> It is significantly more difficult for the cross-cultural counselor to counsel Christianly and effectively. In addition to evaluating the theories and approaches germane to his own cultural background and training, he also has the burden of evaluating counseling approaches indigenous to the client's culture.[8]

The effectiveness of Christian cross-cultural counseling depends on experience, training, and ability of the counselor. Cross-culturally trained guidance counselors are in demand, as our population throughout the U.S. becomes more culturally diverse. "Effectiveness in Christian cross-cultural counseling as in all cross-cultural counseling, depends upon the ability to correctly identify and interpret universal, group—specific data[9]." It has been my experience that what is important is that the counselor has the training and ability to correctly identify and interpret group—specific data and idiosyncratic factors brought to the counseling situation. The task is great but can be mastered.

I realize the task ahead is demanding, but this frontier must be conquered with all vigor, to bring more understanding to this branch of counseling that has been overlooked for years. There are those within the counseling profession that believe a counselor is a counselor, demonstrating their lack of sensitivity and understanding of cultural differences. This article may shed light upon the kind of thinking that hinders the cross-cultural counseling effort to emphasize the need for more qualified counselors in this area:

> On the one hand, there might be a tendency on the part of culturally uninitiated counselors to conclude with Robert Burns, that a man's a man for all of that and proceed on the assumption that people are the same wherever one meets them. On the other hand, once the counselor becomes immersed in a new cultural study, he is apt to conclude that people are so different as to make effective inter-cultural counseling all but impossible. Both extremes are to be avoided.[10]

Juvenile Delinquency and Guidance Counseling

Juvenile delinquency is a topic most guidance counselors would rather not talk about. School dropout rates remain high throughout the country especially in

Florida. When kids are not achieving, they usually find a way to attract attention to themselves. After these attempts fail, they leave school.

There are many reasons for delinquency. The roots of this malady in many cases lie within the family as Ishee states in this example that:

> Jimmy was the youngest of five children, and in a way he had been the pet of the entire family. He had three older brothers and a sister. The sister was the second oldest child, and the boy nearest Jimmy in age, was four years older. All the older children tended to spoil Jimmy when he was young.[11]

The above behavior of Jimmy seemed of no consequence while he was young and the older children thought it was cute. As the child grew and problems of deviant behavior became known, concern grew within his family and with his teachers and counselors. Families may allow behavior that is deviant to go unchecked until it mushrooms, and since the family was large by today's standards, may be why so much was occurring within the family hierarchy that Jimmy's conduct went unchecked.

In some instances it has been my experience that Guidance Counselors and Teachers often are substitute mothers and fathers when the family does not shoulder its responsibility. In some school districts, truant officers monitor school attendance. God, working through Christian counselors, helps to give them the strength to deal with the truant child. Sometimes this child or adolescent may have physical or mental limitations.

Counselors should be trained to find these problems A referral to a school psychologist may be indicated. Jimmy has physical limitations as Ishee indicates:

> Jimmy lacked the natural ability of his older brothers. He was sturdily built, but he was not quite as big as the other boys. A more serious handicap was his lack of hand-eye coordination. He lacked the ability and hand-eye coordination that marks outstanding athletes.[12]

Discipline: Internal vs. External Locus of Control Relevant to Guidance Counseling

As a child grows, he gains a sense of right and wrong, what is valued as good and what is valued as unacceptable behavior to society. From early childhood the evaluations have been going through the child's mind. How parents evaluate a child's behavior and give feedback and the manner of discipline when required determines to some extent whether the child or adolescent develops an internal or external locus of control. My Children experienced this process. In this example:

If Tom has internalized the rules set down by his parents, and does not try to usurp parental authority, his chance of developing an internal locus of control is good. That is, Tom has internalized the rules, mores, and cultural norms of his parents and will be inner-directed, able to function without being directly controlled by parental authority. Gradually, parents will allow Tom to make more of his own decisions based on his inner control of self. On the other hand Bob may continue to be rebellious, though they are concerned parents who have tried to be good examples for Bob to follow. He continually has to be directed by his parents and teachers, and has developed and external locus of control.

John Ishee talks about motivation:

> In studying adolescent motivation, one should bear in mind its dual source, which includes frequent and powerful prompting from within and the situational stimuli of the adolescent's social milieu both of which mold and direct his energies and arrives into adequate or inadequate patterns of activity and experience.[13]

Conclusion

I believe that both environment and heredity work to mold and shape a person's behavior. It is not the environment alone, nor the inborn nature of the person, but a combination of both. School guidance counselors have to deal with these students in spite of their differences. The Christian counselor has a place in the school setting, and in counseling sessions with the student, can appropriate God's grace, the third force in the counseling process.

2

The Third Force in Premarital Counseling

To Live in Love: A Premarital Counseling Challenge

Tammy and Tom scheduled a premarital counseling session with me. They are both 22 years old, college graduates and from middle income families. Tom is impatient, introverted, a perfectionist; Tammy is patient, outgoing, and untidy with her room. Tom keeps his room very neat and clean. They are both Baptists and attend the same church.

During their first counseling session, I began by asking both of them to complete a personal profile. The differences, perfection, imperfection, tidy; untidy; patient, impatient; outgoing, introvert; were evident. As I touched on these differences, Tom and Tammy became aware for the first time that they needed to talk about how they could live with each other in a marriage. Tom wanted the house neat and clean, and Tammy did not place these values high on her list of priorities. I pointed out to Tom that no one is perfect and that trying to be so, may cause problems for him in the marriage, always striving and unable to achieve perfection. It would also be a problem for Tammy since she is untidy. The couple compromised and agreed that Tom would do his best and not feel guilty about his problem with perfection and Tammy would be more careful and pay more attention to keeping the house neat and clean. Tom agreed to work on being more patient. As a child, Tom had a father who was an impatient perfectionist. These tendencies had contaminated his personality. "Tammy's mother was a poor housekeeper, was affected by modeled behavior.[1]"

With counseling and modeling the desired behavior, this couple was able to see themselves and each other in a better light and form a more realistic view of how to love and help each other and overcome their shortcomings. God in their lives made compromise easier.

Is a Courtship Analysis Helpful?

In talking to other Pastors and Ministers, it is a common practice among churches and denominations to have the bride and groom go through premarital counseling before the Pastor marries the couple. Some Pastors counsel once with the bride and groom, whereas others do a series of counseling sessions. I know that several sessions are needed to cover all areas that the Pastor, Minister, or Counselor should work through. Many young people wanting to marry have not evaluated their situation. They have not thought about career choices, their financial situation, their transportation needs if both work, etc. A careful, considerate, caring Pastor or Christian counselor, could help these young people examine the whole picture of their physical, financial, and spiritual needs. In this way, the couple would understand their responsibilities and obligations, and not have to live from one crisis to another.

Many young people enter marriage in a dreamlike state, believing that because they love each other, everything will fall into place. Most of the time things fall out of place because of a lack of correct instruction and planning. This is how most young adults walk into marriage; they believe that:

> To live in the love that was given in the beginning, is to believe in rainbows, and the promise given that mankind will not be destroyed. To live in love is to enter into dialogue encounter with other people and all of existence. To live in love is to experience personal wholeness and integrity. To live in love is to trust the external spirit, to listen when it speaks, to act when it calls, which is every minute of the day. To live in love is to be awestruck by the wonder of how it all is interrelated-oceans crashing on the shore, yellow mustard fields blooming after the first spring rain, wind moaning through giant pines, a dog barking loudly to protect its master, the eyes of the sick, hurt, and lonely, pleading for acceptance, the innocence of the infant reaching out in trust and the tenderness of a hand responding with I love you.[2]

Love is a many splendor thing and to be swept into the ecstasy of it can be breathtaking. The above description is idealistic but at times we have to work toward the ideal to make marriage more enjoyable. The dreamlike state of existence within the marriage can work some of the time, but a solid plan for marriage can make this a reality.

Open and closed people are described as:

> Living in love being difficult or impossible for encapsulated people. Living in love is a lifestyle for those who are dialogically oriented. Encapsulated people

wear rigid armor to keep themselves in and others out. Dialogic people are open and transparent. They believe in self-disclosure and accept disclosures of others.[3]

If the husband is a closed, encapsulated person and the wife is open, dialogically-oriented person, a problem may be on the horizon. The open, transparent wife may have difficulty with her closed husband who is trying to shut out the world. Her husband imprisons himself and by locking his door of communication to his wife, placing her in his prison-cell. Though she may have healthy relationships outside her marriage, it is not the same as being able to relate freely with her husband.

Their marriage could become estranged very soon after the vows are spoken if this problem is not discovered and dealt with during premarital counseling. It may be that during the course of premarital counseling, the coupled will realize that they are too different from each other and are not compatible. They may realize they should not marry. On the other hand, they may be able to work through their differences and maintain a happy marriage. It may help the engaged couple to read good books on how to improve married life, and how to evaluate your girlfriend or boyfriend before fully considering marriage.

These words are timely as:

> Martin Buber, theologian-philosopher, claims there are two kind of people—image people and essence people. Image people are primarily concerned with the impression they make on others. Image people are like overly adapted children. They continually wonder what others are thinking of them. Essence people, in contrast, simply give of themselves, knowing that their basic responsibility is to respond. Their external personality boundaries are permeable, so they move to dialogic encounter with all spheres of existence[4]

Image people carry a burden because they always wonder what people are thinking about them, whereas essence people are open and outgoing, transparent, with nothing to hide. The enclosed person on the other hand, is trying to manage his life in such away as to give the impression he is highly efficient in his work. This kind of person may be high in achievement, but low in loving ability. There are reasons for this kind of behavior and personality slant. These words may enlighten encapsulated people because: "In many marriages, one or both may be image people. They shut off from each other because of fear, guilt, resentment, or disinterest, or because they were adapted in childhood to keep their distance[5]."

Is Listening Essential to Learning for Young Adults

During the time youths are thinking of marriage and possibly going through premarital counseling, they need an ear to listen to them. This is a time when parents can be friends. At times they need a sounding board, As you listen and the children watch your responses, something valuable passes between parent and child. A closer, more trusting relationship may be established during this quality time. My wife and I were always listening even before our children reached the premarital stage. At times, it was up to my wife because I was away on military duty.

Even though children are fast approaching maturity, they continue to seek attention, counsel, and guidance from their parents. Narromore states that: "Even though teenagers are nearing physical and intellectual maturity, they still need a good deal of parental guidance and support. This includes the setting of specific limits and responsibilities for their best welfare.[6]"

Engagement: The Time for Premarital Counseling

At the time of engagement, premarital counseling should be started, unless it is a very early announcement. when engagement is near:

> Some power in man compels him to run away from and get rid of himself. It drives him to want to escape from his own presence. Loving means achieving something, being filled with a spirit which is related to one that inspires artists and priests. It is creation like the work of the poet or prophet.[7]

This is the time of reflection for the couple but there can be pitfalls. These words are instructive:

> Love is definitely a product of culture and can in no sense be called an instinct or an appetite. In love, the individual emerges as a distinct person; in a purely sexual relationship the individual is not important.[8]

I want the couple to plainly see the difference between sex and love. In premarital counseling, this should be brought out. At times, the same word, love is used to describe the infatuation of teens. "When both partners are in agreement that a marriage should take place at a more or less definite time, more emphasis will fall on physical compatability.[9]"

Some may advocate premarital sex, however, it is my view that this should be avoided because men tend to lose respect for women after intercourse, abstinence is best. It is also against God's law.

In the words of Adams, "Premarital counseling must be early, educational and preventive. It consists largely of the work of establishing and encouraging the growth of proper attitudes toward marriage, based on scriptural principles.[10]"

> Then the: Pastoral Counselor is qualified to help the engaged couple because the pastor, as counselor, as well as his role of preacher and teacher, in God's providence is uniquely able to function effectively. His position as one who also is a teacher and preacher of God's Word, enables him to work preventively as well as remedially.[11]

Premarital Counseling with Couples Marrying Outside Their Faith

Another area of concern that must be mentioned is marrying outside one's faith. Pike states that:

> Most people think of the problem as ante-nuptial; they think of it as a clumsy predicament imposed upon a young couple in love by organized religion by denominational differences. It is generally assumed that if these problems can be surmounted one way or another, if some modus operandi can be devised or quite simply, if one party or the other will yield. Then the couple will live their married life as any couple who did not have the problem to solve in the first place.[12]

A research study showed that people marrying outside their faith were more than twice as likely to divorce as an interfaith marriage. We will examine this problem more in depth, because the situation is serious when you have more than a 16 percent divorce rate in 1990 and more than 25 % in 2004because:

> If only your church did not take the view that it does, or if you simply go ahead and sign the papers—dear, everything will be all right. But as we shall see, the reason that organized religion does create the ante-nuptial contracts, is that there is a problem in the marriage itself. Thus we will make better sense out of the premarital problem if we will examine more closely, the married life of couples of different religious persuasions.[13]

Married life between two people of differing faiths does create additional problems within the marriage. Apparently some of these concerns cannot be worked through since the divorce rate is higher among those who marry outside their faith. Pike sheds additional light on the divorce rate:

> There is a fallacy of the isolated illustration. Here we must be realistic because this matter is usually bypassed by such remarks as—Aunt Minnie and Uncle Joe have not had trouble, they simply agreed to disagree and in fact are one of the happiest couples I know. Anyone can readily find some couple of his acquaintance who will serve as the model for such a comment.[14]

It is my belief that a few marriages outside the faith may appear healthy, but if they are examined in depth, some real barriers to a healthy relationship will surface. Many of the by-laws and rules in one denomination may conflict with another, causing turmoil between husband and wife. These problems should be discussed during premarital counseling. There may be conflict about who should do the premarital counseling or where it is to be held. Studies have been done to assess the differences of inter-faith and intra-faith marriages. The numbers:

> From what is called the Maryland study we learn about the religious connection of the parents of twelve thousand young people, and whether their parents were living together or not. The study was sponsored by the American council on Education with the title: "Youth tell their story" and with Dr. Howard M. Bell as the author and compiler. The figures show that where both parents were Protestants, using this word in its customary broad sense, 6.8 percent of the parents were separated. This and all other figures would have been higher were not childless marriages excluded by the nature of the study. Where both parents were Roman Catholics, 6.4 percent of the parents were separated. In the case of mixed marriages, 15.2 percent represented broken homes. Where the parents had no religion, 16.7 percent of the homes were broken.[15]

In the above quotation, it is evident that in mixed marriages, the divorce rate is significantly higher than when Catholics marry within their faith and Protestants within their faith. The highest divorce rate was among those couples who did not profess a religious faith. Premarital counseling hopefully would reduce the number of divorces across all denominational boundaries. Many conflicts can be resolved or eliminated through premarital counseling.

Peer Pressure: Its Effects

Peer pressure is a major concern for parents with drug and alcohol abuse prevalent in this society, but Narramore reminds parents "the starting place is to realize peer influences do not have to be negative and harmful.[16]"

Associating with peers who have good intentions, and whose parents have raised them properly can help to solve the problem of influence. Another child can model the desired behavior for his peer who may internalize these new qualities, habits, etc. For example, "during adolescence, teenagers try out new social roles. They are learning what it is like to choose friends and build relationships.[17]" These new social roles and relationships are part of growing up and becoming an adult. Premarital counseling for those planning to marry is another coq in the wheel helping young people make a crucial adjustment into a new world that is foreign to childhood and some adolescents are more mature than others. Parents, who are concerned and thoughtful, can help their children in these formative and impressionable years of physical and mental growth.

Peer pressure will exact its toll on some youth who are weak and disobey their parents or who have had inadequate parental discipline and training. Narramore continues:

> Few things strike more fear in the hearts of parents than the possibility of peer pressure. We look around at adolescents in our neighborhood or the local school and quake inwardly at the sight. Some are hooked on fast cars and dangerous drugs. A gang of slovenly youths hangs out at the local fast food outlet. Some of the girls wear exceedingly seductive clothes, and others run around dropping a steady stream of profanity from their lips. Parties abound, As well as drugs and violence.[18]

When parents see youth exhibiting the above behavior they are fearful because they have children or grandchildren who could go astray from the way they were taught. At times, peer pressure can be stronger than all the teaching of discipline, morality and responsibility. Peers are with each other more hours in the day than parents and have free time to influence their friends.

In the past ten years, I worked with adolescents at a state facility. It is sad to see young people who have wrecked their lives at such an early age. In many instances, their parents did not set a good example. In such cases, social workers insure that the child is taken to a safe place until a responsible, person, foster home, or responsible relative can be found. If these youths could spend time in a church with good teachers and be taught Biblically, the Spiritual influence would make a difference in their lives. This is a time when they are so easily led astray by peer pressure and other environmental influences.

Conclusion

God is that third force in premarital counseling who is gracious and loving. During the time of courtship, a couple may become so involved that they fail to distinguish love from infatuation. It is important for parents to listen to their teens when they talk. These youths are struggling for identity and toward maturity. By listening to children, we send a message to them saying, I respect you. At the same time, the child will respect adults for being understanding, caring persons. Adolescents need guidelines and discipline. They would rather have boundaries and limits.

Engagement is a time when premarital counseling should begin or it may have begun before this time. The point is that the couple should be counseled about maintaining communication in their marital relationship, managing money and distinguishing between love and infatuation. They also need to be counseled if they marry outside their faith. They need to be aware of peer pressure and its positive and negative consequences. The Apostle Paul wrote: "Children, obey your parents in all things: for this is well pleasing unto the Lord. Fathers, provoke not your Children to anger, lest they be discouraged (Col. 3:20-21).[19]"

3

The Third Force in Marriage Counseling

What Happens after the Honeymoon?

Marriage inevitably reawakens many of the emotions of early family life. The whole community, state, and nation, gain by stable family life. "For the physical and emotional well-being of children, a settled, happy family life is all important.[1]" The emotions that a man has for a woman are conditioned by his early relationships with his mother. It is the feelings that he had for her that he will unconsciously attempt to re-experience in his marriage. "A woman's choice of a husband will also be influenced by her childhood emotions about her father. The opposite could happen, and she may look for a man she can mother, or she may emulate her mother in her marital relationship.[2]"

Even though our choice of marital partners may seem conscious, unconscious elements are at work. If at any time these emotions get out of control, the couple may seek marriage counseling. However, if the couple seeks premarital counseling, the likelihood of having to go to a marriage counselor would diminish. Controlling the emotions is most important. A cutting remark made to the spouse in the heat of an argument, may never completely heal unless the couple is God-fearing and appropriates His love to help them return that love to each other. For the scriptures tell us: "Husbands, love your wives, even as Christ also loved the church and gave himself for it."(Eph.5:25),[3]"

I am commanded to love my wife. Wives are commanded to love their husbands. This Christian love is tender, understanding, and patient. If husbands and wives love each other, not infatuation, but love each other genuinely with the love of Christ in their hearts; the need for marital counseling diminishes further.

It is natural to wonder what happens after the honeymoon. This is where reality puts the rubber to the road. The ceremony is over; the wedding has passed, and the crowds have gone home. It is time for the couple to sit down and say, where are we; where do we go from here?" It is better if the newlyweds have already planned their next step. The husband and wife begin to learn about the nuisances and bad habits of their spouse at

This time these words are descriptive:

> Why can't couples predict adjustments before they get married? We have already seen that their romantic perspectives often blind them. Also, there are adjustments about habits they would not know about, before marriage. He tosses and turns at night; she hangs pantyhose in the bathroom, he throws tools into messy disorganized drawers. These can usually be worked out by compromise.[4]

I advocate compromise and communication as keys to a happy marriage. Many times couples fail to communicate and hold what is hurting them on the inside until it becomes a time bomb ticking inside waiting to explode without warning. In marriage, there are times of boredom, times of dearth:

> Wright declares that: A marriage has its dry moments and hot moments, its ups and downs. Most marriages today do not make it. I think the ones that do, survive by going through these changes. As long as you are allowing something to happen within your marriage, then I think there is some chance for survival. There has to be movement.[5]

Problem Marital Behavior Patterns in Marital Counseling

Problem marital behavior patterns are ignored usually during courtship, and engagement, but after the excitement is over the little problem behaviors begin to appear. If husband and wife are not in real love, they will begin to irritate each other with little habits that annoy. These words are timely; when marital relationships begin to crumble, couples complain about various aspects of their marriage. Bernard Green reported a study of 750 couples complaining of marital problems and he derived the following list of common complaints:

Infidelity............Lack of Communication
Constant arguments............Conflicts about children
Unfulfilled emotional needs............Domineering spouse

Sexual dissatisfaction............Suspicious spouse
Financial disagreements............Alcoholism[6]

These are some of the problems that cause marital conflict and depending how these concerns are dealt with, whether resolution of the conflict is achieved, more dissatisfaction, separation, divorce, spouse abuse or other dire consequences could follow. A couple in marital conflicts should seek help, whether secular or Christian counseling. If one or both were Christians, a counselor of their Christian faith would seem more preferable. The use of God's influence in the lives of counselor and client would be the additional force mediating in and through their hearts to effect personal growth.

In many cases I will be counselor and teacher because many husbands and wives do not know how to communicate or solve problems. They must learn that no marriage is perfect and that they will always need to seek solutions to various situations. The married couple may not need a counselor if they have other couples in whom they can confide. They may already have a wealth of experience in solving marital conflict.

Improving Communication between the Married Couple

Improving communication between husband and wife is the most important avenue to solving marital conflict. If Jane and Tom do not talk to each other, how can they ever agree to disagree? At times emotions are pent up and need release, or Jane and Tom need to talk. Jane has had a very frustrating day at the office, and when she came home, every little thing she asked Tom to fix and he had put off for months, came to mind when he walked through the door. Jane lit into Tom, venting her frustrations by telling him how sorry and undependable he is. Tom, who had a tiring day at work because Friday's are always busy, screamed back at Jane. Both lost self-control verbally. Now they are living in the same house and not speaking to each other. Jane makes a delicious Sunday dinner, sets the table, and calls Tom. After he sits down, she smiles, takes his hand and says Let's talk.

Husband and Wife in Marital Conflict

When I am preparing to counsel a couple about conflict in their marriage, the session may be touch and go initially until rapport is developed and I have had time to piece my observations together Because as Wright declares:

> What you do and the direction you take from here, will vary because of the different responses from each couple you counsel You may want to expand on the responses of each spouse individually in order to understand how their marital problems developed over a period of time. A question like the following can be helpful: think back to when your marriage began having difficulties. What happened to make you feel that way, and what did each of you do about it?[7]

I have to fashion my techniques to the situation at hand. I may counsel husband and wife together initially. After counseling with the couple, it may be necessary to do individual sessions because there may be blocking. Both may be holding back information, hating to hurt each other. Then joint sessions will be required. In these sessions, since I have the background information relative to the root causes of their problems, I will be a catalyst for change by finishing sentences that both husband and wife may be reluctant to finish or may be too painful.

Using this technique two or three times will cause the couple to become more open and transparent in their interactions with each other and the counselor. Then too, the marriage counselor serves as teacher, helping John and Mary to sharpen their problem solving and communication skills. The counselor should encourage openness and candor between the couple. When problems are held inside, John and Mary experience frustration and hostility. By sharing problems and concerns with each other, they share the burden. John and Mary may discover they do not have a problem, and they only needed to talk.

Marital conflict comes from many directions, it may exist because two people came from different cultures. Marilyn and Tony met in a nightclub and were married two weeks later. She came from a middle class family and observed Christian values and mores. Tony came from a different cultural background. The second generation, born in the United States. Though born and raised in the U.S., his family retained their cultural heritage, mores, values, and customs. He, too, was born into a middle class family. Problems came into the marriage because for Tony marriage was a conquest. In his culture it was permissible for a man to have girl friends after marriage. In Marilyn's culture, this was considered infidelity. When husband and wife is in marital conflict:

> One of the axioms that can be applied to marriage is that any difficulties carried by the individuals into the contract will certainly not be improved by the marriage. They will probably become worse. Nervous tension, inadequate preparation, ignorance, or any other of the ills that mankind is heir to, will grow worse in marriage and will compound the natural difficulty that any two people find in learning to live together. The problems of society around us impinge on each one of us as persons, and it is blindness not to see how this adds to the burden we bring into matrimony.[8]

I see difficulties carried into a marriage as weights that hold the couple back from achieving long and short-term goals. Newlyweds may bring a host of bills into the marriage, bad credit, or a poor work record. These problems may be a time bomb that is ticking away, waiting for other problems to overcome the struggling couple. A family with financial problems may find it wise to contact a credit counselor and set up an appointment to work through the problem and set up payment plans for unpaid bills the credit counselor may be able to get the monthly payments lowered, and consolidate others. If Tom and Mary were in marriage counseling and their therapist heard the theme of financial problems mentioned again and again, would probably make a referral for Tom and Mary to a competent credit counselor. Another one of my jobs is to make appropriate referrals when required.

Nervous tension, inadequate preparation, and ignorance, are some of the ills that can overpower a couple because these problems were brought into the marriage. A marriage that had its genesis without problems, will in time run into, as sailors call it heavy weather. When a couple marries without adequate resources, they have already set up themselves for failure. Though some of these marriages will not fail.

However, they will be highly strained, and this could breed other problems such as violence, abuse, and much unhappiness.

I have seen some couples who enter the marriage door blind and ignorant of what to expect. Not only will they be lacking financially, but also they will not have the benefit of premarital counseling or family support. Some low-income families, though they lack financially, will save money for special events in their lives, such as marriage. They have strong ties to their church and have the benefit of close ties to their Pastor. They also have strong family ties and support. Low-income couples with this type of support system usually have strong Christian beliefs and would receive counseling from their Pastor. Bob and Nikki was such a couple. They saved a nest egg for the expense of their marriage to purchase appliances.

On the other side of the coin, I have seen the low-income family, third generation, on food stamps, no reliable work history, and a poor credit history. Jim and Shirley are from broken homes. Both Shirley and Jim do not attend church, have a busy nightlife, are promiscuous, and have a dim outlook on life. They believe that life is stacked against them and they intend to get everything they can without working. Jim and Shirley decided to marry after she became pregnant. Jim does not have a steady job and Shirley works for temporary services. They will not have a wedding ceremony or seek premarital counseling, entering marriage broke, blind, and ignorant of the consequences likely to follow.

When love and marital conflict are hot topics of discussion, those involved think how tangled love affairs can become with some reaching out for love and never touching or tasting its nectar. These words by Thornton Wilder are timely:

> She had never realized any love save love as passion. Such love, though it expands itself in generosity and thoughtfulness, though it gives to visions and great poetry, remains among the sharpest expressions of self-interest. Not until it has passed through its own self-hatred, through mockery, through great doubts; can it take its place among the loyalties. Many who had spent a lifetime in it can tell us less of love than a child who lost a dog yesterday, The Bridge of San Luis Rey.[9]

In the above quote, I see Thornton Wilder assessing love as something with fleeting characteristics and hard to define or describe. But he states that a child who lost his dog yesterday, probably knows more about love than the anonymous woman who only realized love as passion. Many people, young and old, could express the same feelings about what they think love is. A child in his innocence and simplicity of thought, is capable of exhibiting love for mother, his or her dog, in a way that a passing stranger would not miss. Love has a fleeting character. But if Counselors have Christ in them, it will be as distinctive as the love the child exhibits for someone he or she cares for dearly and deeply. The third force in the counseling triad who powerfully edifies in Christian counseling.

Some types of husbands and wives a marriage counselor will encounter, may be described this way:

> As counselors, we have seen them, the woman dowdy, depressed, without make-up, without self-respect, often tearful; quite certain that she is useless and unlovable and has no right to expect anything good. She is often married to the destructive, critical, sarcastic type of man who has reduced her to the state she is in, or so it would appear. The male counterpart of this type is similarly depressed and defeated. He is often sexually impotent, which is his unconscious revenge against his dominating, overbearing, condemning wife. Clients of this type visibly blossom, particularly the woman, after a few interviews. Their improved appearance and attitude often reduce the partner's unconscious anxiety to what his destructiveness has done and he can restore some love to the marriage.[10]

It has been my experience that when married couples destroy each other's loyalties, self-confidence, and self-worth, both lose a sense of direction in their relationship. In this case, the woman had lost her self-respect, and did not care about her personal appearance; her emotions were on the surface. She is described as domineering, overbearing, and condemning. It seems that this kind of behavior toward her husband caused him to react by being critical, destructive, and sarcastic, or it could be that this was his personality makeup and her actions brought the worst of the husband's behavior to the surface. A Christian marriage counselor could help them realize change, improve appearance and attitude with the husband and wife, and restore love and interest to the marriage.

Edifying and helping are involved in counseling. Galatians 6:2 teaches the concept of bearing one another's burdens: "Bear, endure, carry, one another's burdens and troublesome moral faults, and in this way fulfill and observe perfectly the law of Christ, the Messiah, complete what is lacking in your obedience to it.[11]"

We are commanded by Scripture to bear one another's burdens, to edify and lift up one another and help each other. When a Counselor is listening to a client, he or she is edifying. This may be the first time in the client's life that someone has really taken the time to listen. From this attention, the client draws strength, self-worth, and a sense that the therapist is a caring, warm, understanding person that can be trusted.

False Ideas about Love Examined in Marital Counseling

The idea that the immature person cannot love is usually thought of as one of the false ideas that recur in marital counseling; however, these words convey this thought:

> The immature person cannot love any more than a newborn infant can walk. The ability to love another person does not exist until the total personality is developed. Then one has the capacity for loving neighbor, white or black, and for loving those of the past, whose shoulders we stand on. To love, one must have the capacity for courage, faith and discipline.[12]

Then, it is evident that only a mature person has the capacity to love. Before one is capable of love, he or she cannot communicate effectively. But with total integration of personality, a person can open the eyes and really see with the heart. The eye of the mind opens with understanding, and a capacity to love. "Many of our people are faced with the same problem presented to their Victorian ancestors, they suddenly find themselves married to a stranger.[13]"

Conclusion

After the honeymoon is over, the couple really gets to know each other. They become their real selves. All the bad habits come out of the closet, but if the married couple leave open the line of communication, they can solve most of their problems.

Marital conflict has many and varied root causes, but most can be surmounted. Problems brought into the marriage may be most troublesome because they are excess baggage on top of whatever new problems occur. Some false ideas about love in marriage were examined. The truth is that an immature person is incapable of love until his or her personality has matured.

4

The Third Force in Family Counseling

Marriage Is for a Lifetime

Thinking of the family, warm feelings of togetherness often come to mind: such as going to church, playgrounds, and picnics. Many times the opposite is true, each person goes in different directions. Unity within the family is a jewel that requires work. For good balance within the framework of marriage, each partner must enjoy interdependence and independence. Many people, who marry, never think about the loss of total independence before they marry, but much thought should be given to this because marriage is a shared relationship.

In a problem marriage, there could be many reasons. However, a couple must learn to talk about what is upsetting or hurting them. If John is angry, but repressing it, he should learn to express to Mary just what she has done to make him angry. Then they can work on resolving the problem by confronting each other, working not to repeat defeating behaviors.

I find it necessary for the whole family to come into counseling at times. There may be an unhealthy way of relating to each other among family members. When the family is no longer functional as a unit, help should be sought to re-establish family unity and a healthy relationship among its members.

It may be that the flame of love is about to flicker out, or the spark has fizzled. These words convey what a dysfunctional family needs to make it healthy again because:

> Coexisting with a need to be loved is a need to love. In loving, we feel that the good within us is preponderant over the bad, and that we have love inside us sufficient to fulfill the needs of a partner as well as our own. Marriage is a great reassurance regarding the good within us; it is proof of our inner store of love.

Sexual relations in marriage are an added reassurance. Many people carry within them, infantile fantasies that the fulfillment of their sexual needs involves damage and destruction. A happy marital sexual relationship is proof to the partners that their sexual desire is in fact a good and loving thing, in that it fulfills and satisfies each other.[1]

I know that marriage is a great assurance regarding the good within us, but when it turns sour it seems as though that reassurance is fleeting and slips away without notice. The marital relationship is an assurance that one is loved and that one is capable of loving in most instances. But when a conflict arises, between husband and wife, and if the children are involved family counseling may be indicated.

Family Counseling to Help Family Members Control Anger

Family counseling may be used to help control anger. It may be that one family member is inciting others to anger. The job of the counselor is to get the family involved in inter-actions that exhibit the behavior that will be examined. Once this is done, the counselor will help the family find and use healthier ways of relating.

Another problem may be in the way the children fit in the family hierarchy. Because one child is older than the other does not mean that in the family pattern of relationships, the older child will be dominant. It may be that a younger child is noisier and, demands more attention from the parents, and runs Roughshod over older, quieter siblings.

The older children may become jealous of the younger child getting all the attention and set up a plan to undermine the younger sibling to get even. When nobody is looking, an older child may push the younger sibling causing him or her to fall. The intent of the older child would be to put fear in the younger which would supposedly make her or him quiet around the house, thereby re-establishing the older child's dominance. But when Jeanie becomes angry and brings the incident to the attention of her mother, Tom is punished. The incident is repeated several times and gets out of hand.

It may be that the counselor will not have to set up a special scenario to discover the cause of the problem. By allowing family members to sit where they are most comfortable, the counselor may draw conclusions based on the seats chosen by each member. The little noisy kid, who has learned how to attract attention, would probably want the seat occupied by an older sibling. This behavior could be repeated, because children find an infinite number of ways to keep their parents occupied. These situations and circumstances may cause family upheaval.

Relationships can be loving and friendly within the family structure, or may be intolerable. It depends on whether the children, and even the parents, are disciplined. In some families, it takes about thirty seconds to discover who is in charge. Children are over talking parents, not paying attention to pleading mothers and fathers for them to obey. In a situation like this, no amount of counseling will help unless parents are in control of their children.

I would make recommendations to the parents. At the top of the list would be a statement to the effect that the parents must establish order within the family, starting with themselves. Children, who are raised in Christian homes where limits are set and there is discipline, will not encounter these kinds of problems. If children are in subjection to their parents, about the only reason for family counseling would be some psychological or psychiatric problem that the counselor, psychologist, or psychiatrist may need to diagnose and implement therapy and training with the family to enable them to live with or overcome the problem. Herbert and Jarvis observed that:

> With so many: relational patterns within a family, among spouses, children, brothers, sisters; some of these relationships are hard to decipher at times, especially members of the family who are indifferent. There are family members who are lukewarm, may be open and friendly at times, and be closed and sullen at other times.[2]

The following may help to identify people who do not fit in the category of open, friendly, outgoing, and caring. Because a "simple way of recognizing a social misfit is by the paucity of the relationships he makes; he either makes none at all or only dependent ones, or hostile ones.[3]"

Problems Brought into the Marriage

I consider Problems brought into the marriage as additional burdens that will strain the family relationship at the worst time. In some marriages, the mother or father or both may bring children from previous marriages or relationships into the marriage to live under the same roof. There could be sibling rivalry. Another problem, the children of one parent may not listen to the other parent because those children know that he or she is not the natural father or mother. The couple will need to work this problem out before marriage is consummated, probably in premarital counseling, because it could be an emotional issue.

There is the burden of alimony that some parents will have to pay from previous marriages, or for children fathered out of wedlock. These are additional problems brought into a marriage that must be dealt with because these concerns will not disappear. The best time to discuss these problems is before marriage. Husband and wife should be clear and frank in their discussions, to avoid later misunderstandings and heartache.

If Paul neglects to tell Tammy before they marry, that he has to pay child support for two children from a previous marriage, Tammy is going to ask questions when his money is less than it should be. When the couple is unable to afford the house of Tammy's dreams, when she discovers that the credit report shows Paul is paying alimony, she may file for divorce.

Children in the Marriage

Children are a blessing, a crowning glory to a marriage. Children add life to a home and to a marriage. Mother and Father are passing through unfamiliar territory when they become parents, because they are charting an undiscovered course and have not had training as parents. I remember the experience of helping my wife raise six children. We grew up with the first three and raised the last three siblings. It took that long to learn parenting.

Train a child in the way he should go is a commandment from God. If children are not trained properly, they will surely go astray and cause tears to flow from their parent's eyes. But if there is discipline and openness in the home, children feel free to discuss what is going on at school and in the community. In this type of home environment, a child will grow physically and intellectually. In a Christian home the child will also grow spiritually with proper direction and teaching in the word of God, along with attending church and Sunday school on a regular basis.

In the book of Proverbs, there is instruction to parents, for the Word says: "Train a child up in the way he should go and when he is old, he will not depart from it.[4]" We should train children to be God-fearing, and under the control of their parents. Then it will be easier to resist peer pressure when they become adolescents. Children will have inner control of self, rather than be externally controlled by peers and others who may be a bad influence on them.

The following words shed light on the difficult task of raising children:

> Despite common assumptions to the contrary, learning how to be a parent does not come naturally. Bringing children into the world and raising them can be a very arduous task. In our society today, these difficulties are often glossed over, because parenthood is more romanticized in America than Marriage.[5]

I understand that Parenthood in the U. S. is held in high regard, but the difficulties of raising children are not confronted head on and resolved. In most families, husbands and wives work and daycare is depended upon to be a surrogate parent. Most families cannot afford to lose the income of a husband or wife who takes an extended unpaid leave of absence to raise and nurture a child.

The task of raising children is arduous; it is continuous during the first few months of the child's life. Some couples do not make suitable parents because they are too impatient. Others want all their time for their own pursuits, while others make a conscious decision to not have children. It is my view that it is better for a couple to decide against having children, than to bring them into the world and abuse and neglect them. If children are abused and neglected, they may become a problem for society at large to deal with. It is best to bring them up in a nurturing, caring home.

Childhood Needs: Unmet in the Family Tree

Children have many unmet needs in the family. Since both parents work in most families, the task of caring for the children is shouldered by childcare centers. These words are appropriate:

> Few Parents anywhere have ever put themselves as hugely and hopefully in the hands of child care counselors, as American parents of aspiring classes have, in the twentieth century. And few parents anywhere have ever had so hard a time raising their children.[6]

Because children are being partially raised by childcare workers and partly by their parents, mothers and fathers are experiencing difficulties raising their children. Whereas the parents may discipline their children, childcare workers may not, or they may not have the authority. Another problem is that childcare centers may use other forms of discipline.

A popular form of discipline in many childcare centers across the country is time out as punishment when a child misbehaves. The child is placed alone in a room for a period of time. Isolation is used as punishment for some children and for those who do not receive adequate attention at home and possibly in daycare, this could be an attention-seeking device. Break a rule or misbehave and a child care counselor or worker will come and put the child in seclusion.

At times children exhibit behavior that borders on being abnormal. For example Cole states that:

> It is quite normal for children to quarrel among themselves. And to make matters worse, they do it loudly. Parents are accustomed to the loud wails of arguments that occur between brothers and sisters, or between children and their playmates. Childhood jealousies over what they perceive to be parental favoritism, their need for love and recognition, and the usual competition between children, are frequent causes of childhood squabbling. All of these things are commonplace experiences in the lives of children and are part of the growing up process.[7]

In the above quotation, I note that healthy children make noise when they play. They are just being children. They are quick to sense unfairness or favoritism in parents. Children need love and recognition because these are powerful stimuli for them to use in developing a sense of caring and love for others. If you have not experienced love, how can you show love to others? When a counselor observes behaviors a child exhibits that are abnormal, a psychologist or psychiatrist should be referred to for evaluation and therapy. These observations would warrant evaluation because:

> What is not normal is when a child consistently behaves cruelly toward other children. When that happens, parents should seek qualified help for their child to determine the underlying causes of his or her behavior.[8]

Qualified help is required because at this early critical juncture of the child's life, corrective measures may be taken and treatment, if needed, can be started. Parents should know that:

> There are no hard and fast rules or guidelines to use to determine if their child has emotional problems or if his or her behavior is normal for someone their age. There are some general warning signs that apply to children four years of age and older. Repeated threats and actions of physical attack against other children. Listen to the child's language when he or she talks about others. If

they consistently speak of wanting to hurt other children, find out why they feel this way. Does the child have a violent extremely angry reaction to other children when they refuse to do what he or she wants? Coupled with this behavior pattern, is the overall behavior mostly anti-social? That is, does the child willfully harm pets or damage property? Examine the child's values and see if he or she has any sense of distinction between good and bad.[9]

The child is to be observed by parents; speech is important. Does he or she talk about hurting others? Does he or she go out of the way to scare or humiliate other children? Does the child have violent, angry reactions to other children when they do not give into his or her will? Is the child mostly anti-social when all behaviors are looked at as a whole? This is why a qualified professional in the field of behavioral sciences should examine any child exhibiting these behaviors.

I believe these problem behaviors are the result of children growing up in a home or environment where there is not enough parental guidance and control. A child may grow up in a neighborhood exposed to gang violence, deviance or truancy. These factors tend to influence behavior for the most part, though not in all cases.

There are other important signs to look for in a problem child. Douglas Cole describes other danger signs compared to an emotionally healthy child:

An emotionally healthy youngster will usually be aware of some moral standard in his or her life and will know the difference between the two. One key factor to observe is whether or not he or she feels any sense of guilt or shame after having hurt another child. The repeated absence of guilt is a pretty good indication that the child is not only operating out of a moral vacuum, but is developing an anti-social pattern which can only cause pain for him and others.[10]

The parent should try to discover whether the child feels shame or guilt after hurting another child. If he or she does not feel remorseful or guilty, or exhibit a sense of shame, may have deeper-rooted problems and may not have a moral code at all and is an anti-social person. A child exhibiting these types of behaviors should be evaluated at once.

Conclusion

Marriage, in the most ideal state, is for a lifetime, until death shall bride and groom part. God working through the couple, if they claim a faith, is able to enhance the quality of their lives. They have a sense of destiny beyond this life. Like it or not, everyone thinks about what happens after physical death. The third force, God in our lives, completes the cycle of everlasting destiny.

When problems enter the marriage of couples who believe in Christ, they can appropriate Him as their helper, whether through a Christian counselor, prayer, or through reading His word. Problems brought into a marriage compound as ongoing situations and concerns develop. Through family counseling, help is available.

Children in a marriage are a special blessing from God. Most parents place more emphasis on their children in the marriage than the marriage itself. Children who hurt other children and show no remorse or shame may be operating out of a moral vacuum, and should be evaluated immediately.

5

The Third Force in Individual Therapy

Should Christians Needing Counseling Seek Secular Or Christian Counselors

I know people who go to their therapist, not so much because of a particular problem in their life, but it could be a floating anxiety, a phobia, etc. At times a person who is in the process of upward mobility, may feel guilty because their status is low in the eyes of society, who have a problem introducing their newly acquainted, upwardly mobile friends as cited in this example:

> I don't know what to do, help? A friend on her job has noticed Jane's behavior change in the past two months and quietly, confidentially asked, are you o.k. Jane? She may have stated, I have a problem because my faith does not practice birth control.[1]

The question is often asked, should Christians seek secular or Christian counseling? Many pastors have begun to rethink the question of referral to secular counselors. The following statement is considered overdue: "The bankruptcy of modern counseling theories, has tended to encourage pastors to rethink the entire question of referral.[2]"

I have talked to Pastors who have become disillusioned with modern counseling theories and consider most of them to be without substance, or Bankrupt. They believe they can do a better job doing their own counseling. Pastors, when properly trained in counseling, are uniquely prepared to counsel, because in addition to counseling skills, they bring a strong faith in God, and power of intercession through prayer and God's Word. God is the third force in Counseling when the Pastor or a Christian counselor counsels a client.

Pastors are reclaiming a job that is really theirs. As long as they are trained in Counseling, I support pastoral counseling by the Clergy for "more and more the idea of counseling as the work of organized religion in general, and the Pastor in particular, has begun to emerge.[3]"

This could prove to be a healthy sign for the church and pastors. I want to make this point crystal clear, that the pastor or minister must be trained before attempting to counsel, because an untrained counselor is worst than no counselor at all. Jesus was the master counselor. He did not use threats or condemnation in His counseling but emphasized love, understanding, and confrontation when needed.

The visible church has not kept abreast in the counseling field and secular agencies and institutions have filled the void. This situation did not occur overnight, but over time the church allowed secular agencies to come in and counsel even church members. Jay Adams comments on the church doing their own counseling:

> To produce the present situation, in which young people can grow up in a Bible believing congregation; graduate from a Christian college, enter a graduate doctoral program, and are never confronted with the biblical truth that counseling is the work of the church. Only in most recent times has there been a healthy change of direction. Conservative churches have been growing stronger, liberalism has waned and there is a new emphasis on the organized church, as opposed to the remnant theology that previously tended to stress the invisible or unorganized church.[4]

Students are going from kindergarten through the twelfth grade and through graduate school and never presented Biblical truth that counseling is the work of the church. But the church is bouncing back, taking their place in this field.

Should Pastors Rethink Referral to Secular Counselors?

I believe Pastors should continue to rethink referral, and prepare themselves academically for counseling if they are not trained. Anderson had this to say about prominence given to psychiatry and psychoanalysis:

> The recent prominence given to psychiatry and psychoanalysis tends to elevate the wise pastors counseling program up to the high professional plane of phy-

sicians and attorneys. Roy Burkhart says that the minister ought to be familiar with the healing resources of psychology and with the analytical techniques of psychiatry. He need not specialize in dealing with the mentally ill, but he will need to recognize the signs of serious trouble; he will want to lead his people in a program of preventive measures, looking to the spiritual and mental health of his people.[5]

The pastor oversees his flock and should be observant and pick up any abnormal behavior of members. He should strive to keep his members both spiritually and mentally healthy. The pastor needs a working knowledge of psychology and psychiatry to keep his people with a sound mind and spirit. Anderson continues:

Pastors should cooperate with professional services just as Jesus combined His healing ministry with that of preaching and teaching, so the efficient pastor should cooperate with physicians in their ministry to the various needs around them. Our best physicians tell us that most physical ills are not merely somatic, but psychosomatic.[6]

I have talked with Pastors who are rethinking referral because they do not want to subject their members to the theoretically empty theories of secular counselors. When counseling a client, the Christian counselor must abide by the principles that Jesus exemplified and must never condone sin. Though the emphasis is on forgiveness, sin cannot be swept under the rug.

The following statement is worth noting that Jesus never condoned sin; neither should we. David Seaburg said, "the basic teaching of Jesus is compassion based on understanding.[7]"

Compassion is the key. If we have this jewel, we have one of the basic skills of a pastor or counselor. Understanding is another virtue that helps the counselor to be believable, so his client fully trusts him.

Should a Counselee Condemn His Own Behavior When It Is Wrong: A Counseling Perspective

When I am in therapy with a client, sin must be dealt with in an understanding manner. When counseling a husband or wife individually or together, the pastor should emphasize the impropriety of sin, and the behavior should be condemned. By condemning sin, the cycle of confession and forgiveness is set in motion. How can a person be forgiven if he or she fails to acknowledge guilt? If the counseled stands firm and condemns his or her own behavior, the client will be set free by telling the truth.

At times a client may become upset and angry. I know at times it is good to be angry about sinful conduct: since "not everything that can be identified under the heading of anger is a violation of God's law, for Ephesians 4:26 instructs us to be ye angry and sin not.[8]

I am convinced there is a difference between strong feeling, and the seething hostility, which is consistently condemned in the scripture. A client should condemn his conduct if it is wrong. This is the first step toward healing and wholeness, the journey to a new person. In Jesus' words, you must be born again. I am talking about repentance. With this in mind, the following is true, that:

> Frequently, a problem is cleared up by repentance when seeking and granting of forgiveness. All is warm and well. But in time, weeks or months later, the reconciled parties have grown cold and have drifted apart. Why is this? Shouldn't reconciliation lead to new and better relationships? Yes, it should, but it will not automatically do so. After reconciling us to Himself in Christ, God then spends much time changing our relationship and us to Him.[9]

When Confrontation Is Necessary in Individual Counseling

In individual counseling, confrontation is necessary to get to the truth by bringing a client face to face with the problem that he or she wants to sidestep. When a pastor, pastoral or Christian counselor cares deeply about a fellow Christian, he will, because he loves Christ and his fellowman, confront a brother or sister to allow them to look reality in the face and see themselves as they are. Then they can move on in the name of God. If the therapist and client is God fearing, they can secure His grace and be set free. Augsburger talks about standing in the clients shoes:

> Pastoral caring means a willingness to stand with others in their confused and angry thoughts, and to value their right to be angry even while not necessarily agreeing with all their angry demands. Pastoral care implies care of the whole person, not just what is agreeable to or affirming for the pastor.[10]

When confrontation is necessary in individual counseling, caring means a willingness to stand with others in a time of need. Even if the client is confused and angry, the Christian counselor will stand by his client and assist in every way possible.

I see Pastoral care in individual counseling as caring for the whole person. What purpose would it serve to treat one problem and not treat the whole person? The client would not benefit if only one problem is solved and two or more are left untreated. The therapist is obligated not only to be agreeable but also to help others face their situations with a plan to make the whole person a productive citizen who is able to turn his life around and live for Christ or rededicate his or her spiritual walk with the Master.

I have discovered that confrontational pastoral care can bring the patient or client face to face with the truth since:

> Confrontational pastoral care can help persons discover that judgment is a vehicle of grace. When faced with considering other perspectives, which often entails some kind of self assessment, parishioners may discover personal limitations, faults, shortcomings and omissions are difficult to face without a sense of the presence of God's grace.[11]

I know that judgment is a vehicle of God's grace. This is how a person appropriates grace, through going to God admitting that I am a sinner and I have come before His judgment seat to ask forgiveness. Personal assessments are good, and have their place, but beyond that where does the suffering Christian or non-Christian go? People are finite, have limitations, faults, and shortcomings. Any self-assessment made by a person in these miserable circumstances would be flawed. When a client needs counseling, he is not at his best spiritually, intellectually, or physically, because what affects one part of the body, affects the rest, since the whole person is in view. It is my belief that the counselor, regardless of his orientation, must take a holistic view of counseling to be most effective.

When a client feels and believes he is at rock bottom and is told by a Christian counselor, you don't have to bear every burden because you are bankrupt in the sight of God. The bankruptcy court judge, Jesus Christ, has declared the burden (debt) lifted off your shoulders and placed on His.' This is the third force at work in the counseling triad. When the Christian counselor and client agree to appropriate God's grace, Jesus Christ becomes their third partner in counseling.

God so loved the world that He gave His only begotten Son, Jesus Christ, for the sins of the world.

Jesus is the propitiation (satisfaction to God) for our sins. God's gift of Jesus Christ to the world is God's grace to us for grace is the outworking of love. God not only said He loved the world, but also put His love in action. Absolute love at the highest level (Agape) is active.

Pastoral and Christian counselors should exemplify the same type of loving, sharing, caring, non-judgmental attitude in their counseling ministry. They should exemplify Christ in their lives, in their moral, spiritual, and emotional spheres. These qualities should shine through their personalities. It is not something they can put on and take off like a glove, but they should be filled throughout, with Christ in their lives.

Conclusion

Christians in need of counseling should seek Christian counselors. If they are members of a church, their pastor may be able to counsel. If not a member, may be helped by a counseling department in a church with qualified counselors. The Christian in need of counseling may have a Christian friend who knows a Christian counselor and make a referral. Referral is appropriate when a Pastor is a counselor but believes he does not possess the skills or expertise to deal with special situations. This may include but is not limited to counseling homosexuals or lesbians who wish to overcome this sin and appropriate God's grace. The Pastor, who is not trained in Counseling, should acquire training unless he knows he is not cut out to do this job.

Should pastors make referrals to secular Counselors? As much as possible, pastors, pastoral Counselors and Christian Counselors should not make referrals. The pastoral and Christian counseling profession is organized at the national and international level. Christian psychiatrists, psychologists, and psychotherapists are board certified. Through referral and by using this network of Christian professionals, Christians can be counseled from this unique perspective with Christ at the center of the counseling triad.

I know it is the right choice to make for clients to condemn their own behavior when it is wrong? To look at self and say I am wrong is therapy in itself. Self-understanding is wisdom. To Appropriate God's help in individual counseling, the person has to admit wrong behavior. In many cases the client will be free of wrongful behavior and is in counseling because someone else has treated him or her poorly. On the other hand, no one may be at fault. Confrontation is necessary at times in the Counseling process to achieve movement and release of information held back by the client. In Christian counseling, confrontation may be necessary to help the Christian come face to face with God's help. In marital and family Counseling, two or more people tell the story, and they confront each other at times. In individual Counseling, only one person is telling his or her story. It is left to the counselor to do the confronting if needed.

6

The Third Force in Mental Health Counseling

Delinquent and Deviant Behavior and Mental Health Counseling

"Susan is feeling depressed, stale, flat, and unprofitable.[1] She has been in a state mental hospital once, but lately has been under the care of a community-based mental health clinic. I was part of the treatment team that discharged Barbara from the hospital and found placement for her. Like Susan, Barbara was depressed. She joined a church and learned about God's grace and its sufficiency and is feeling better now. She grew up in a strict religious family, and when Barbara was five years old, her father and mother kept telling her God sees everything you do and will punish you for doing bad things. Barbara became frightful and never overcame these feelings. While in counseling with her pastor, he told her about the love of Christ, that it is His will that none should perish. This was the first time Barbara had heard of God as love.

Delinquent behavior can be tied to mental health because this type of behavior usually has its beginnings in childhood. Roger Smith states that:

> In attempting to uncover the roots of juvenile delinquency, the social scientist has long since ceased to search for devils in the mind or stigma of the body. It is now largely agreed that delinquent behavior, like most social behavior is learned and that it is learned in the process of social interaction[2].

When I am counseling delinquents, I must remember what I am dealing with. I am not dealing with devils in the mind but learned behavior. If Robert started skipping school in the third grade and is now in the tenth grade and has moved on to more deviant behavior such as stealing cars and breaking into homes, It may be impossible to rehabilitate him at this late stage. If the counselor could have involved Robert and his family in turning him around in the third grade, there may have been hope. This would have required total effort from the school counselor, probably another counselor trained to deal with deviant behavior, parents, and truant officers. Early intervention is the only way a child can be rescued in most cases. Vice has to be dealt with before it becomes habitual.

Criminal or deviant behavior involves a learning process, and once the learning has taken place, the offender believes he or she is smarter than the criminal justice system. Once Robert turns to a life of crime and is initiated by hardened criminals, it is usually too late to rescue him. Every effort should be made to ensure that children are in school and not on the streets learning to become criminals. The following statement conveys the beginning process of the downward spiral to a life of crime:

> The classic statement of this position is found in Sutherland's theory of differential association, which asserts that criminal or deviant behavior involves the learning of techniques of committing crimes, and motives, drives, rationalizations, and attitudes favorable to the violation of law. Unfortunately, the specific content of what is learned, as opposed to the process by which it is learned, has received relatively little attention in either theory or research. Perhaps the single strongest school of thought on the nature of this content, has centered on the idea of a deviant sub-culture, it is argued, is a system of values that represents an inversion of the values held by respectable law-abiding society.[3]

I have counseled clients with delinquent behavior that involves learning the craft of thievery, lawlessness, and attitudes that are counter to good order in society. Further, delinquency is described as fostered by a delinquent sub-culture. These are people who have placed themselves outside of the dominion of respectable, law-abiding society. Intervention at an early age is the solution with something meaningful: a job, job training, a mentor-someone or something to fill this void in an unproductive and unfulfilling life.

Depression: And Mental Health Counseling

Mental health counseling involves many different facets, as patients' complaints will be varied. The most common problem is mental depression. Kline draws a picture of this malady:

> Depression is the most common of all psychotic ills. Fortunately it is also one, that as a rule, heals quite readily in treatment. That statement may surprise many, including some who now suffer from the malady. In the course of a varied psychiatric practice, I have treated more than 5,000 depressed patients and the majority of them have achieved good recovery.[4]

In my counseling practice, I have seen how the hope of getting better is therapeutic and like a breath of fresh air for the person suffering from depression. In this pastor's situation cited in the reference below; he was humiliated to have to check into a mental hospital and come face to face with one of his members. Don never forgot the words of a counselor that he met when he first arrived. This description brings focus to the story:

> You'll get better, it will take time, but you'll get better. I'll always be grateful for those gentle words-profound in their simplicity-yet filled with hope. And oh, how I needed hope. For one brief moment there was a slight glimmer of light in my black hole of depression, not much light-not enough to discern direction, or illuminate the many unanswered questions.[5]

After Don felt a glimmer of hope, he was profoundly grateful for those gentle words. Though these words were so simple, their meaning was profound. It was like a jolt of electricity out of the blue. Those words lifted Don ten feet high out of that deep, dark hole of desperation and hopelessness. Yet Don had many unanswered questions. He was concerned about what would happen to him, his family, and his congregation. He was disillusioned as these descriptive words reveal and Don is telling his own story:

> I had lost touch completely with reality. God was not real, life was not real, love was not real, my wife was not real, my children were not real, friends were not real, I was not real. All life was pretense and fantasy, I thought.[6]

In my mind as I read about Don's situation, I can picture how life was not real for Don because he had lost contact with reality, but everything else was. Don's coping mechanism was at work protecting his real self from what was happening to him. But, in time he would get better.

> When dealing with depressed patients: the therapist in many instances can recognize depressives on sight. The inner anguish that afflicts them is signaled in many ways by small, outward signs, such as dress, posture, gait, and manner.[7]

I think it is something all co-workers do is to assess each other's skills and at times situations occur that exposes them. I have kept mental notes thinking who I would want to represent my patient in court if I could not attend. One of the most important tools in the hands of the mental health counselor, Pastor or Minister is their diagnostic ability. To be able to recognize the little mannerisms: dress, posture, gait, and the inner feelings of anger trapped inside begging to get out, crying out for help. These tools aid the counselor in developing a treatment plan for the client. I have identified mental health patients-pointed them out to my wife while in a restaurant or while walking in the community. It is interesting how the untrained eye and mind will miss these little clues that are so apparent to those trained in mental health, behavioral sciences, psychology, and psychiatry.

Kline describes his method of breaking the ice with patients to let them know the doctor has spoken. He states that: "sometimes it makes it easier for the patient when he or she is first seen, to ask, are you depressed.[8]"

A psychiatrist, psychologist, or therapist can save time by being specific. The key is, be sure you know what you are talking about. To convey the idea you know what you are talking about builds interest and hope in the client. Kline further states that the following counselor statements convey this idea when he says to the patient, "you seem depressed". He conveys the thought that he is thoroughly familiar with the problem and that "he sees in it nothing odd or unusual and certainly nothing to occasion guilt or shame.[9]" This is another way of letting the patient know that the counselor is with him or her and that I am walking with the patient in his or her shoes. The Christian or non-Christian needs this kind of support and assurance.

In the mental health field, the psychiatrist is the expert who prescribes medication if needed. Kline, speaking from experience in his practice, says:

> For nearly all depressed patients, I prescribe medications designed to correct or compensate for chemical imbalance. In simple, uncomplicated cases this eventually relieves the symptoms and ends the matter.[10]

When a patient's depression is not serious, medication may be indicated if counseling alone will not lift the depression. If there were a chemical imbalance, a counselor would be correct in making a referral. Medication relieves the symptoms in some cases, but it does not deal with the underlying problem. Kline talks about more complex cases:

> In more complicated cases the medication relieves the depressive symptoms, but does not restore the deeper-rooted psychotic problems. As the consultation develops, some other problems may emerge. The patient may have some conflicts with his children, indeed with himself. He may be neurotic, though not necessarily so. He may need psychotherapy, though again not necessarily.[11]

I have seen times when neither medication nor counseling alone improves the patient; a combination of both was the answer. A referral is appropriate whenever the counselor is in doubt. The counselor may have a working agreement with psychologists and psychiatrists.

Environmental stress is of major concern in mental health. At times a Christian will become stressed out because he or she holds problems inside without the benefit of sharing these concerns with a friend, spouse, or counselor. Before long, it becomes a crisis. In Ephesians chapter four, the word of God reads:

> Let not the sun go down on your anger. This woman had let many moons go down on hers. That is why she had an ulcer; it was not because she was mentally ill. It was not because others were responsible for this ulcer; but it was because of the sinful patterns of responding to wrongdoing that she had developed over the years.[12]

Mental Health Counseling and Environmental Stress

My experience is that many that come to their Pastor or Counselor are not mentally ill or defective in their thinking. The problem is that they have tried to hold everything inside and not dealt with real problems in their lives that will not simply go away. The wife who developed an ulcer after keeping a list of offenses her husband had committed against her is an example. Rather than try to discuss the problem with her husband, she chose to make a list. She let the sun and moon go down on her anger many times. This dysfunctional relationship finally took the form of an ulcer.

Stress often manifests its long-term effects through physical problems. Even when Mary thinks she is suppressing her anger, it is quietly at work causing other physical problems. It behooves Christians and non-Christians to be sure they do not carry burdens around but seek help. Help may be a quiet chat with a trusted friend, a talk with the abusive husband, or formal consultation with a counselor. At times; the Christian or pastoral counselor will refer the client to a medical doctor. Some of the counselor's clients will be in therapy and under medical treatment at the same time.

Christine Baldwin believes in journal writing as a tool to release tensions and pressures. She draws a mental picture relating how change is difficult for some people to deal with:

> We are living in a culture that views change as threatening. We are taught to perceive life as linear, implying a destination. Change is perceived only as an intermediary process on our way to this idealized stability. But no matter how we are raised to view life, life is change. To see change as a normal condition of life goes directly against the myth of destination, yet meshes more perfectly with experience. When we see change as the normal condition of life, we stand in revolt against the expectation of a final goal for our lives and cease to view process as threatening or temparary.[13]

Baldwin views journal writing as a useful way of releasing tensions. I think a person writing for release of worry and tensions may write about anything that comes to mind as Baldwin did. It seems akin to daydreaming, the difference is that the journal writer is writing down thoughts. Different approaches work for different people to release the stress, which is a consequence of living in a fast paced society.

The Role of the Church in Mental Health Counseling

I see the role of the church in mental health counseling as clearly defined. The pastor, who Stands on Sunday morning performs group counseling. Members find a release of burdens and are edified by the pastor and others during the service. Members are peer counselors for each other. These words are timely:

> Churches have always been major contributors to personality health. As Karl Menninger has observed that Religion has been the world's psychiatrist throughout the centuries. Without the stabilizing, undergirding, nurturing

value-supporting ministries of the churches, millions of persons in every age group, would have been diminished in their abilities to handle life situation constructively.[14]

I commend the church even in this generation because it remains a beacon of light, a refuge and a stabilizing force, an underpinning for society. To some families, the church is a mother for the motherless, a father for the fatherless, and a bridge over troubled waters. As Menninger stated, religion has been the world's psychiatrist.

Jesus was the greatest counselor the world has ever known. A prime example is when the people brought the woman caught in adultery to Him. He listened to the accusers, posed a question, bent over, and began to write on the ground. After some time, He looked up and the crowd was gone, none were without sin. "They have not condemned you, neither do I, go and sin no more."(John 8:10-11,)[15]"

The Pastoral Counselor: With Mental Health Training

Clergymen have contributed to the mental health profession over the years. "Their most significant direct contribution to mental health is their counseling and shepherding of troubled persons.[16]"

The Apostle Paul encouraged his son in the ministry to: "stir up the gift of God that is in thee, for God hath not given you the spirit of fear; but power and of love, and of a sound mind[17]."

What is the pastoral counselor's role in mental health? The pastoral counselor or pastor, if appropriately trained, is uniquely qualified to effectively minister to the mental health of the congregation. The goal is to keep the flock endowed with a sound mind.

These insights are enlightening: In all cultures physicians and personal counselors or directors, have played their parts side by side. Very naturally, the guides of souls have used medical analogies. The sickness of the soul and its healing were prominent concepts of the ancient world. In platonic dialogues, Socrates regards himself as a physician of the soul. His conversations exhibit a method of psychiatry, or soul healing, though the term may not be applied here in its modern medical sense. For Socrates, men's souls are sick chiefly when they are victims of erroneous thinking.[18]

In my studies in and about the mental health field including its history I find that for centuries, men's souls have been ministered to by physicians, counselors, poets, and others who do things that help people look beyond themselves. They have ministered to the soul those things and situations, which cause mankind to come together in a oneness, such as a city taking pride in self; its football team is a rallying point for its citizens. The doctor always engages in therapeutic small talk while treating his or her patients. In this way the physician administers therapy to the physical body as well as the spirit of the patient, and both are nourished.

When people go to see a play with all the actors putting on their best and brightest performances, there is something about the actors performances that is bigger than the physical person. It is the soul, through self-expression, mannerisms, or ways of being, which mirrors a reflection of who they are. The soul for man is often referred to as the immortal part as expressed in these words:

> In the apology, Plato has Socrates declare that, at God's bidding, he has gone about exhorting old and young to care for their bodies and for money more than the welfare of their souls. The soul for him was the immortal part of man; the mortal body was its instrument in the present life.[19]

For Socrates, the soul is the immortal part of man, his body is a house for the soul in this life.

Conclusion

The third force in mental health counseling is God working through men to care for His people. God is also the third force in the Christian counseling triad. Delinquent and deviant behaviors are learned and usually the school for acquiring these types of behaviors is in the streets of the city. The best time to get a handle on delinquency is when it starts in elementary school with counselors, parents, and truant officers working together.

Depression is the most common malady encountered in mental health counseling. It is not difficult in most cases to get under control or in remission, as medication or counseling may be indicated. Environmental stress takes its toll in a fast paced society, but with professional help it can be controlled.

The church has been the great counselor of the ages for the masses that have continued to hold out hope beyond hope The pastoral counselor is especially qualified to help the congregation maintain their mental health, if he or she is professionally trained. In the counseling session, with concurrence of counselor and client, God is invited into the door to add his blessing to the counseling triad.

7

The Third Force in Crisis Counseling

When the First Crisis Comes in Counseling

John called his therapist at four in the morning: "I cannot go on any longer, life is not worth living. But I will be all right tomorrow. John's therapist, Paul, assured him that life is worth living, though at times people have distressing problems.[1]" Paul asked John where he lived and said he would be there in five minutes. Paul did not want John left alone. After he reached his client, he talked to him about Jesus' love for him and asked John to go with him to the mental health section of the local hospital. "There is no emergency more dramatic or more draining, than that which surrounds the threat of or attempt at self-destruction.[2]"

When the first trial comes in crisis counseling for a therapist, he or she will come face to face with life and death if the client is suicidal. Hopefully it will be a counseling situation that is less serious. But a Doctor or therapist learns to handle an emergency by dealing with an emergency. These words are eye opening as Clinebell describes:

> The art of reflective listening is essential in counseling. The pastor attempts to listen to feelings as well as words. He listens for feelings that are between the lines, feelings that are too painful to trust to words. Now and again he responds to these feelings.[3]

A good counselor is valuable to his or her clients and has mastered the art of reflective listening. The counselor listens for those feelings behind the words too painful to say. At times, the feelings are such that the counselor may read between the lines.

There are times when one looks back to a miserable period in his or her life that shows courage was displayed in spite of the circumstances. Viktor Frankl looked back to such a time in his life and declared:

> Reflecting on his death camp experiences was to him who saw no more meaning in his life, no aim, no purpose, that he was soon lost. In crisis ministry, the clergyman's role is to awaken meanings, which is crucially important. His unique function is to help crisis-stricken people rediscover the ultimate meaningfulness of life lived in relationship with God. His steadfast love is real and available even in the midst of tragedy.[4]

In positions of deacon, pastor, chaplain and counselor, I have counseled and consoled church members and others who were sick or lost loved ones. I vividly recall the hot day in summer when I came on duty as Chaplain. I received a call from the chaplain coordinator who asked me to come to the tarmac quickly because the family of a patient requested prayer before their love one was transferred by air ambulance to a trauma center. The patient had sustained a severe head injury. Members may call on their pastor to share with them or their family or counsel to relieve grief or feelings of loss. Life must go on, and life must always be worth living. Frankl had the same kind of experience in the death camp in Germany. Woe to him, who saw no more aim, sense or purpose in his life. When faced with life's threatening situations, sometimes the difference between those who survive and those who perish is their determination to live or lack of inner strength. A saving knowledge of Jesus Christ will give a Christian that assurance.

When the first trial comes in crisis counseling, the counselor needs the undergirding of God permeating his or her life. These words convey protection: "and His name shall be called wonderful! Counselor.[5]" and "where there is no guidance, a people fall; but in an abundance of counselors there is safety.[6]" God can renew and transform his people. The Apostle Paul, a counselor who settled many disturbances in the Churches he planted, declared, "and be transformed by the renewal of your mind.[7]"

In the presence of counselors there is safety, but where there is no guidance, they will suffer. Christians are to be transformed by the renewal of their minds. This is done through the study of God's word, prayer, and meditation.

When the first crisis comes, the counselor should have in place a network of referral sources on which he can depend. These resources should include the poison control center, emergency room, crisis center number for the public, and mental health professionals. When an emergency comes, there is no time to get ready, you must be primed to go. I remember medical emergencies I was involved with while serving as a hospital corpsman in the United States Navy. Waiting to put on the coveted Chief's Anchors, it seemed that the waiting from the time I received the news, until I was promoted, as if it were an eternity. During this time, several medical emergencies occurred. I often wondered if an improperly handled emergency would jeopardize promotion.

The ultimate test came while on the third leg of the flight from Quonset point, Rhode Island to Diego Garcia, located in the Indian Ocean, an 11,000-mile journey. While in route from Yokota, Japan to Bangkok, Thailand, one of the men suffered a myocardial infarction. As senior corpsman on the flight, after examining the patient, I started mouth to mouth resuscitation and external heart massage, then gave oxygen. Two corpsmen were on the flight helping care for the patient.

The Pilot of the C-141, star lifter troop transport summoned me to the cabin to obtain pertinent medical information. I gave the pilot the patient's tentative diagnosis, vital signs, blood pressure, temperature, respiration, and a brief medical history. Then the pilot said, check his arms and legs for drug abuse. This pilot had been flying in and out of Viet Nam where there was drug use. There were no signs. The pilot then radioed the nearest U. S. base located in the Philippine Islands and made an emergency landing. The ambulance and medical personnel were waiting when the plane landed. I was blessed to have the help of the Chief personnelman aboard the flight.

Upon landing, he advised me that a report should be sent to home base at Quonset Point, Rhode Island. With this accomplished, the flight continued on to Bangkok, Thailand; then on to Diego Garcia located in the Indian Ocean.

Years of experience and preparation with other emergencies had prepared me for the emergency of a lifetime. Another important link of preparation was attending the coveted, advanced hospital corps "B" school in 1965. It is located on the grounds of Portsmouth Naval Hospital, Portsmouth, Virginia. This school is required for Corpsmen serving aboard ship on independent duty without a Medical Doctor as well as other independent duty assignments. All Corpsmen involved in this lifesaving event received commendations. Crisis counselors must be ready; they do not have time to get ready when a crisis comes.

I know that developing a relationship with the client or patient is most important for the crisis counselor as indicated in Clinebell's words:

As the parishioner senses even vaguely, that the minister is really trying to listen deeply and to relate fully, a tiny fragile nexus as delicate as a spider web, will begin to connect his aloneness. This is the first vital strand of what will become a sturdy bridge connecting the islands of awareness of two human beings. This bridge is called rapport.[8]

In the process of getting to know each other, a sense of trust is formed in the mind of the client or patient. Without this relationship, the crisis counselor will not reach first base. If in a crisis the client and counselor cannot relate to each other, a referral should be made immediately. If a life-threatening situation exists, the police or another public service center counselor needs to make sure the client or patient does not leave. If the person is able to relate to the counselor in a life-threatening emergency, the therapist will be able to get his or her client or patient to a clinic or hospital. During this time, the client or patient should not be left alone.

Where Inspiration Comes into Crisis Counseling

There is a time when inspiration will keep the Christian counselor and client in harmony as stated in Crane's book, Where God comes in:

Inspiration can be thought of in several ways. It implies that there is something spiritual within a person, which motivates him to respond. Another idea is that one is breathed into. When we think of the work of the holy spirit And the nature of spirit itself, we realize that inspiration means that which is breathed into a person, it is like a breath of life, something that is truly inspiring, rejuvenates, revives, and motivates. Therefore, when we speak of the Counselor providing inspiration, it should be clearly understood that the counselor has nothing to give unless first it is given to him.[9]

If a Pastoral or Christian counselor does not come to the counseling session with something given by God, the therapist will not bring inspiration to his or her counseling. Where God comes in, in Biblical counseling and the power of His spirit, the Holy Spirit is at work. This is what makes the difference between Bible-based and secular counseling. I hasten to point out that it is not the label placed on the counseling, it is the counselor and his relationship to God that determines if his counseling is secular or Christian.

Suicidal Emergencies: What Has to Be Done

In suicidal emergencies, there are things that must be done very quickly. The Threat of suicide is what I will address. Over time the counselor will counsel with his clients during several appointments. If there is any doubt in his or her mind during the session or after that a client or patient may be thinking of suicide, the counselor should take precautionary steps to ensure the client, or patient is not left alone.

I may call a friend to be with my client if I am going out of town. I would also give my patients or clients a phone number where I can be reached and let them know who to call as my back up. This is assurance to persons in stress to know that there is always someone they can depend on and call for help.

When a Christian is in counseling with a Christian counselor, they have God as their strength. This scripture points out that:

> There is no trial that has overtaken you but what is common to man, and God is faithful, who will not allow you to be tested beyond that which you are able to bear, with the test, will provide the way out that you may be able to bear it.[10]

When dealing with emergencies that could result in suicide, care should be given to find out from the client or someone close to him, that which led up to the attempt to commit suicide. Maybe the client was upset about something that was not his or her fault. It could be true guilt about something the client did of which he or she is ashamed. A client may be a victim of false guilt. False guilt is as destructive as true guilt if the person involved thinks he or she is guilty before God. Even if a Christian was mistaken and uninformed concerning this point, if he or she knows about the sufficient grace of God from a biblical point of view, and God's power to forgive through His grace which is Jesus Christ. The client could, with this knowledge, untangle the spider web. This would set the person free in his or her own mind even though the person is already free, the difference is that he or she does not know this.

An illustration may help; if the person attempting suicide had sent Tommy to the store and Tommy was struck by a car, became paralyzed, and his father John feels guilty every time he looks at Tommy—thinking he caused the child to be paralyzed. The truth is, as long as John did not have any wrong motives in mind when he made the decision to send Tommy to the store, he would be suffering false guilt. If on the other hand, John was angry with Tommy, and sent him to the store to punish him, this would be true guilt.

Jay Adams illustrates how God is everywhere, even in a crisis:

> Since God is in the crisis, all language and thought that the crisis is beyond limits-is too much or impossible and so on are wrong. But when we size up a crisis biblically, we discover that it is of limited extent; it is limited by God's will. As Job discovered, it can achieve only His purposes, and nothing more. Furthermore, consider this important fact: every crisis is limited by the faithfulness of God to his children.[11]

I see through the prism of biblical history that mankind, from the days of old, has seen the power of God manifested. Through his mighty works: the Israelites walked through the Red sea while God's mighty power held the waters; God delivering Daniel from the lions den, and many other mighty works demonstrating His omnipotence and sovereignty. God cannot be limited. You can limit yourself. No one created Him and God spoke and creation of the universe became a reality. Job discovered how God controls everything, for he tasted both goodness and bitterness while being tested.

Suicide and Method of Prevention in Crisis Counseling

Suicide is a reality in society, and it touches every age group; young and old, every class, rich and poor, and every race and ethnic group. Belief in a supreme being, if a person has God in his or her life, the chance of committing suicide is less than those who have not developed a philosophy for life that believes in a supreme being and an afterlife with God. This is why Christian counselors in the church, school, and workplace are needed more than ever to help stem the tide of suicides, rapes, murders, and many other crimes that defy description.

Seriously suicidal people should never be left alone. The crisis counselor should have a network of helping professionals to ensure he or she is never left alone without backup. Left alone for few seconds, the seriously suicidal person could kill. A warning flag should go up when a client who has been apathetic with little or no improvement in therapy, suddenly seems as though he or she is at peace with the world. The person may act as though all worries and problems have been solved. He or she may have conceived a plan to commit suicide; planned a way out of the dilemma.

I know a technique the Christian counselor can use to diffuse thoughts of suicide that the client may have. This is a valuable tool to help the suicidal patient think about other lives he or she would touch, embarrass, hurt, and disappoint. The counselor may even be able to convince the client that suicide is a selfish act in light of the other people involved indirectly.

These words describe a way of helping the seriously suicidal person look at the consequences of his or her behavior, in this preview:

> In speaking with a person who is a serious suicidal risk, we may endeavor, as MacKinnon and Michaels suggest; the psychiatric interview in clinical practice, to help the individual express in the interview the same emotions that the suicide will symbolize. Then, the person's own control will be able to operate more effectively, and the need for committing suicide will be lessened.[12]

There will be clients who come for counseling or may already be in therapy who have attempted suicide before. What the pastoral, Christian or secular counselor must bear in mind is that some of these clients will attempt suicide again. These descriptive words come from two authors, Everstine and Everstine, who have hands on experience and declare that:

> The person who has made a serious suicide attempt is at considerable risk of making another potentially more lethal attempt in the future, and the defense of denial, or even reaction-formation, can be strong in many cases. A wise clinician will be on the alert for these defenses and will make use of therapy to put them into perspective. It will be necessary to ensure that none of the reasons for a previous suicide attempt still apply.[13]

I understand that the person who has attempted suicide will attempt to do it again in some instances. As the consultation develops during the counseling session, may be able to make use of therapy to help put the client or patient's thoughts, and defense of denial into words that will help defuse the previous reasons for suicide. The counselor must be alert at all times and be a true friend to the client to draw out the very substance of his or her thoughts, aspirations, and problems. Many thoughts may be too painful to put into words, so the counselor must be alert to the following questions: does facial expression match verbal expression? Is there hidden hostility in his or her voice, panic or apathy? What is his or her relationship with family and friends? What is the quality of the relationships with family? And, does he or she have friends.

A survey form that will draw out this information when the person first comes to therapy is helpful. However, a wise counselor may attach these questions to something the client says in the therapy session. It may be a sentence the client or patient started but found too painful to finish. The counselor, through experience and practice is able to couch his words to make their impact constructive and healing.

Narramore tells how guilt troubles so many people. These words are a reminder of how critical and crucial suicide prevention is because:

> In depressed persons I have encountered the harsh, self-condemning attitudes that drive 21,000 United States citizens to suicide annually. As I gained clinical experience, I began to recognize that more people were troubled by guilt than I had realized. Their guilt was hidden. I found that some people who were never able to get their act together and achieve academic, vocational, or marital success, were troubled by guilt. Feeling undeserving of success because of guilt, they repeatedly involved themselves in situations doomed, by selecting mates who repeated the neurotic relationships they had with their parents or previous spouse.[14]

In the above quotation, Narramore is saying that many people feel guilty because they have not lived up to the expectations of others. They also feel that they have not lived up to their own expectations, because they, in the eyes of their parents, do not fit the mold of high academic achievement that the smith family is known for. They feel guilty because they just cannot get their act together. One failure or perceived failure in their lives sets up another. On the other hand, the person may be repeating learned self defeating behavior that parents passed on to him or her during the formative and impressionable years of childhood. It may be that all Tom wanted to be was a wildlife ranger for the state or National Park service. His parents wanted him to be a doctor or lawyer.

Tom's mother sticks pain and frustration in his mind by making remarks such as I wanted you to be a doctor like your daddy. This kind of little off hand statement tends to frustrate. Many times mom and dad do not realize what they are doing when they needle their kids. Children want to be loved by their parents especially when they believe and feel the whole world is against them, at times.

Conclusion

When the first crisis comes, what the Christian crisis counselor brings to the job in terms of knowledge, wisdom, experience and practice, will determine how effective his or her counseling will be. Inspiration is what God has wrought in the counselor's life in terms of regeneration. If the counselor has really accepted Christ as his or her personal savior and his or her new life has permeated—the therapist's counseling ministry, the counseling can be described as inspired. The style and substance of one's counseling cannot be better than the kind of life the counselor lives.

In cases where the potential for suicide is great, the client should never be left alone because only a few seconds can make the difference between life and death. One method of suicide prevention is the clinical interview where the therapist asks the client or patient to describe his or her method or methods of suicide. This tends to diffuse the idea of suicide when the client gives his or her own pre-view of self-destruction and has time to think about the consequences of his or her actions in terms of its impact on self and others.

8

The Third Force in Counseling the Terminally Patient

When One Fears Death and Seeks Counseling

When one fears death, usually after learning he or she has a terminal illness, the client may seek counseling. Some hospitals operate a hospice though these are not commonplace. I can think of at least two hospices in the Jacksonville, Florida area. One, which I am more familiar with, is Methodist Hospice located in the Hospital complex.

Its most important function is to help the patient understand that he or she must come to grips with the terminal illness and that it is better to enjoy the precious time left instead of allowing self-pity to hasten death. The hospice staff (doctors, chaplains, counselors, nurses, and others) have as their major goals the integration of medical treatment, family involvement, and counseling with chaplains. Pastoral care, comfort for the whole person, and most of all, to give the terminally ill patient the dignity and respect the client deserves.

To fulfill some of the dreams of young people especially, hospice counselors will plan a trip to Disney World, Wild Waters or Six Flags over Georgia, etc. For children who are facing eternity without the benefit of experiencing life, this has a twofold effect. It brings happiness to the child, the family, and he or she is able to experience joy during his or her last days on earth.

Most terminally ill patients, when the news of their condition is broken to them by their doctor, refuse to accept it and may get a second or third opinion. These words are typical of how most people react to news that they are terminally ill. "Among over two hundred dying patients we have interviewed, most reacted to the awareness of a terminal illness at first, with the statement, "no, not me, it cannot be true.[1]" The first reaction is denial, the next in many instances, is to seek a second opinion. I remember when my former pastor was ill though the church did not know he would never return. His family took him from hospital to hospital, seeking disproof of what the first had told them.

After a second opinion confirms the terminal illness, the next reaction is the patient's anger. If he or she claims to be a Christian, the patient may become angry with God and ask why have you cheated me out of life? I'm not ready to die yet.

These are typical responses that the patient will make to his or her doctor, chaplain, or Christian counselor. What puzzles me, is that some Christians who claim to be living close to God in terms of a spiritual life try to back away from death when it knocks on their door. It may be that stepping off into an uncharted sea where no travelers return to tell the pilgrim about the journey on his or her way to this eternal voyage is frightening. It. may be they doubt their salvation.

Hospice chaplains and Christian counselors can help patients with God mediating through the therapist, renew their faith and confidence in God. Once the patient comes to the realization that he or she is terminally ill and there will be no reversal of course, that the ship has set sail for all eternity, the client's anger, frustration and disbelief will gradually ebb away into an understanding of his or her condition. These words by Ira Tanner are appropriate: "grieving intensely is no more an indication of a weak faith, than is grieving lightly a proof of strong faith. Many believers deny their grief reaction.[2]"

In counseling with the terminally ill person, the patient's grief reaction has to be dealt with. Many will deny grief; many will deny hurt and disappointment though it may be just beneath the surface. The alert Christian counselor will work diligently with the patient and family in taking them through the grief process brought on by the revelation that their family member is terminally ill. When the patient dies, the family will go through another grief process.

After the Christian counselor is well into the therapy, which includes the pastoral counselor and other counselors whose counseling has a Biblical base, not only by their professing but by the way they live, may use reminiscence therapy and allow the patient to look back over his or her life. At times, a person's life has been so troublesome and turbulent that he or she may not want to look back. Rather, may want to concentrate on doing some fun things to enhance the quality of life experiences in his or her final days. The counselor will need to continually assess the relationship with the client because it is possible for the patient to regress. Feelings of sadness or anger may return. This is a time when a patient could be suicidal. Who may reason to self that since he or she is dying anyway, might as well end the suffering.

If the patient feels close to his or her family and does not feel or believe that he or she is a burden to them, will be less likely to commit suicide. During grief counseling, there may be tears; emotions may run high, or there may be suppressed grief. Some Christians repress their grief because they believe it is a sign of a weak Christian to become emotional. This is not a sign of a strong faith or weak. These words shed light on the grieving process and its impact on the patient and family as Soulten describes how:

> It helps to talk and it even helps to cry, is the statement of a very grateful patient. It is the last statement made by Mrs. Butler to her pastoral counselor. Before this, of course, is the anguish of the troubled soul who is in the process of dying and who thus finds herself in the loneliest situation known to man. Whatever the medical reason, she has arrived at the point of death and now finds that there are few people to whom she can communicate her experience of dying.[3]

I see how it helps to talk and cry when going through the grief process. Crying and talking are necessary to achieve release of anger and frustration, and move on to enjoy those final days with family and friends. In some cases very old persons have outlived their contemporaries and life is lonely and empty. This is another type of patient to observe closely as potential suicide risk Their friends are gone, often alone and neglected, they feel left out and left behind by society. The hospice team considers these factors. Hospice is a friend to those who have outlived their friends. If the patient is at home, hospice will sometimes send out volunteers who will talk with the patient, is a friend and run errands and do other helpful things. Fearing death and now in counseling, the patient will share the good and bad experiences that he or she has gone through. In the latter days of his life, David had a talk with God through prayer:

> In his prayer, in the book of Psalms, the psalmist, King David cried, Hear my prayer, O Lord, and give ear unto my cry; hold not thy peace at my tears; for I am a stranger with thee, and a sojourner as all my fathers were. O spare me that I may recover strength, before I go hence, and be no more.[4]

David said, hear my prayer oh Lord, and listen to my cry. In tears he said, I am a stranger with you and just traveling through the earth as my fathers did. Allow me to regain my strength before I go and be no more. I believe David wrote those words in his old age when his blood was thin, when his steps were halting, when King David knew the end was flashing before him. The following statement warns ministers and pastors against complacency when dealing with families who are grieving: "We are more than technicians, yet, just because grief is our specialty, we must studiously avoid becoming technicians of death[5]." Many ministers who do not make follow-up visits to the family after their loved one is buried are technicians of death. They do not give the warmth and caring a family needs while mourning the loss of their loved ones. The family needs their pastor more at this time than right after the funeral. These comments build on the expression, which signify that some ministers are technicians of death when:

> Ministers who perfunctorily make two or three visits before or after death, and who perform expected rites and ceremonies at the funeral and at the grave, have become technicians of death. This is one way of handling the problem of grief. But such ministers are not true to their calling.[6]

The phrase technician of death comes up again. This kind of attitude within the ranks of God's servants is not acceptable. Grief should be dealt with. The pastor, associate or deacon does not have to do that much, just be a friend, a shoulder to lean on in this time of need for the grief stricken family. Hospices have a follow-up process in place whereby they maintain visits with the family for up to a year after their loved ones die. This enables the family to go through the grief recovery process. This long process requires time. Not all-family members will experience inner healing at the same rate. It will take some longer than others. The word of God is needed to nurture people, and families, back to wholeness.

The Pastor, and His Function in Helping Members Understand the Grief Process

These words are absolutely true that: "Grieving persons need the ministry of the word of God and nothing less than the word.[7]" Pastors should minister the word of God to these grieving souls who do not need a funeral director.

Grief counseling is more exclusively a pastor's than any other form of therapy that he may give. Yet many are neglecting to do it, and the people are suffering. A clear picture emerges from Jay Adam's who says:

> A pastor does no counseling that is considered more exclusively his own than the counseling of people in grief. If grief is peculiarly within the minister's province, all of you must be deeply interested in the nature of grief and what

God wants you to do to help grief sufferers. As ministers, you and I need to do much thinking about grief, and it is also our task to speak and write definitely about this matter.[8]

I know that God wants His ministers to help grief sufferers through counseling, prayer, and by sharing His word with the bereaved and be a friend. The hurt, the pain, and the sorrow must be dealt with. It must not be allowed to remain trapped inside grieving families. Most secular counselors cannot deal with grief as effectively as a Christian counselor. Having the word of God to share with the grieving and being a Christian counselor helps deal with clients from a position of strength. Standing on the foundation of the Apostles, on the foundation of the church Fathers, and standing on the foundation of all the forerunners in the great Christian tradition is the strength and power of the Christian counselor, when he or she has God permeating through his or her life.

Understanding Loss in the Grief Process

Understanding loss in the grief process is a hard pill to swallow for family and friends. In considering the enormity of the problem, Edgar N. Jackson says: "Grief is a universal human experience. It is the strong emotion we feel when we come face to face with the death of someone who has been a part of our lives.[9]" The experience is global; it is a time when people come face to face with the movement of man through the last stage of human life. During the grieving process, a strong emotional response is experienced. A spouse dies, the husband or wife may follow in a few days or months especially if they had a close attachment to each other.

Struggling to understand loss in the grief process requires patience and a caring, sharing, nurturing attitude by the pastor, congregation, and friends.

Tanner focuses on the pain of grief:

> And, needing to express grief we feel such a desert inside, a poverty that the deepest and truest things about our feelings will stay unsaid, stretching beyond words. The more deeply we grieve the larger our agony of non-expression. Words grow fewer, finally there are none.[10]

I have performed in all of these roles and the Christian counselor will play many: a grief counselor, mental health counselor, marriage, etc., but in grief counseling, just being with the person or family is most important. The inexperienced counselor may ask, what do I say? Most of the time, the family will need to talk to reflect on their loved one's life; what he or she was like; how the person fit in as part of the family, or how he or she really loved kids or loved baseball. With grief counseling, it is responding to what is said and using counseling skills to foster insights, to be a friend. Many times when a family member grieves deeply, there is no need for words. Touching or holding the sobbing, agonizing person in your arms will convey the deeper sense beyond words.

Inner Healing of Pain and Loss in Grief Counseling

Inner healing of pain and loss is a slow process. I was district seven leader at my church for three years prior to being called to the ministry. During this time several deaths occurred. As an ordained deacon, my job was to visit the family member during sickness, and in some cases if death occurred, spend time with the family. Because of the close follow-up I maintained with the sick members, the news was not surprising. In most cases a year after the death of a loved one, the family continued to suffer residual grief.

Whether the loss is final or expected because the patient is terminally ill, the process is the same. The exception is in the terminally ill, for them the family often continues the grieving process.

Ira Tanner draws a picture of what the patient and family will need to rest the verdict on in that:

> Physical and emotional healing require three things; information, validation and confrontation, Crystal clear information on the facts of healing, facilitates the healing process. Enlightened patients, who know what to expect, heal quicker than those with little or no information. Think of grief as a healing process through which the fact of loss, and loss "is made real to us." Knowing what feelings to expect, that grieving the loss of a pet, of friendship, is normal, that self-pity is not abnormal, that anger is common, clears up fear and ignorance, allowing the grieving process to flow naturally.[11]

Family members want a clear set of facts that can be confirmed by other physicians. I feel better if I have two or three opinions that agree, if the opinions are independent. Confrontation, coming face to face with the reality of death, helps clear the mind and rest the soul on the finality of the situation.

Tanner continues on the importance of validation:

> It is required for sound mental and emotional healing. The word validation means confirming or making sure. Informed by the doctor that we have a terminal illness with six months to live, we will in all likelihood, seek validation of a second doctor, maybe a third.[12]

After the patient accepts validation, he or she begins to trust his or her feelings and in:

> Loss, we tend, you see, to be distrustful of our loss feelings, particularly a traumatic loss. We cannot fathom what is happening to us, maybe it is not happening at all. We need others, their listening, words, sheer presence to validate our reaction, assure us that yes, the loss has indeed happened, that yes, we can trust our feelings of loss.[13]

Religious Faith and Loss

Religious faith and loss is sometimes a paradox because:

> Grieving intensely is no more an indication of weak faith than is grieving lightly a proof of a strong faith. Many believers actually deny their grief reaction, believing God loves them only when they are nice or joyful.[14]"

You cannot judge the depth of commitment by religious faith or by a person's reaction to grief. If a person lives close to God and has developed a philosophy for life, the overall grieving process may not last as long as for someone who does not know God.

Somehow grief and anger must be worked through because:

> We need to give God our grief anger. In the Old Testament, Job, upon loss of his family in a violent storm, hurled anger at God. God understood, for the Bible says, grieve but grieve with hope. We do blame God for some of our losses, we should not feel guilty telling Him we are angry.[15]

When we cannot deal with the problem, we should give it to God. He is able to help.

Conclusion

When the terminally ill patient first comes to counseling, he or she is seeking help to alleviate the pain of grief. The patient is probably wondering what death is like. The counselor will try to determine if he or she can bring calm to the grieving family. The fear of death, especially to the terminally ill, may evoke anger because the patient may believe God has been unfair because He is shortening the patient's life.

Loss of a loved one is especially hard to understand if the person is a child whose life is swept away before he or she can enjoy it. Inner healing of pain and loss is the goal of the Christian counselor. To the extent that young children can believe and trust God, they will be able to find a way out of their misery. If the pastor is faithful to his members in taking them through the grief process, he will not be a technician of death.

I am certain that religious faith is helpful as preparation for coming to an understanding that life on earth is only temporary and we are sojourners waiting to go home to a place not made by human hands. Grieving will not be more or less for the Christian because there is hardly any difference in the process. Many Christians think grieving is a sign of weakness. When a person has accepted Christ as personal savior, the patient, church member or client will be able to accept death more readily.

Synopsis

Looking over the entire scope of this script, I believe that our Children addressed in chapter one are so important that by whatever means and at whatever cost, they are worth saving. They are our future, our Nations future. Premarital counseling is most valuable to the couple anticipating marriage. In this way they can examine their relationship through the guidance of a Trained Pastor, Therapist, Christian Counselor, Psychologist, or Psychiatrist, who perform counseling. The key is to gain insight about the relationship and work through problems and concerns.

The Family is the basic unit that, depending on its state of health, determines whether our society stands or falls. For this reason family counseling, when needed will insure that, father, mother, and the children will become a healthy unit again. In individual counseling, confrontation by the counselor becomes necessary at times to facilitate movement in the session. The client may be blocking, holding back information, or some problems or concerns may be too painful to put into words. In pre-marital and marital counseling, the couples confront each other. Then work to resolve and compromise.

As we look at the final three chapters: mental health, crisis, and counseling the terminally ill patient, we begin to realize that life is a journey that requires adjustments. Sometimes, treatment of mind, body and soul is required. In chapter six, the one malady that is most common to mankind with respect to mental health is depression. The purpose for this chapter is to encourage the maintenance of a healthy mind. In this life Crisis will come and as the keeper of God's flock, the Pastor will help his congregation maintain spiritual, mental health, and at times, deal with peoples lives that are in crisis. Grief should not be left trapped in a patient, client or family who has lost a loved one. Terminal illness of a family member will cause the patient and family grief that through counseling and spiritual support of the Pastor, congregation, and Christian counselor, begin the journey back to wholeness in the spiritual, mental, and physical spheres.

References

Chapter one

1. Viktor E. Frankl, "The Will to Meaning". (New York: New American Library, 1970), p. 15.

2. Justin Pikunas, Eugene J. Albrecht, and Robert P. O' Neil, "Human Development" : A Science of Growth".(New York: McGraw-Hill Book Co., 1969), p.265.

3. Ibid

4. Ibid

5. Ibid

6. David J. Hesselgrave, "Counseling Cross-Culturally" (Grand Rapids: Baker Book House, 1984), p. 145.

7. Ibid

8. Ibid

9. Ibid

10. Ibid

11. John Ishee," When Trouble Comes". (Nashville: Broadman, Press, 1970), p.268.

12. Ibid

13. Pikunas, et. al, p.268.

Chapter two

1. Muriel M. James, "Born to Love". (New York: Bantam Books, 1970), p. 201.

2. Ibid, p.204.

3. Ibid, pp.204, 205.

4. Ibid, p. 205

5. Ibid

6. Bruce Narramore, "Adolescence is Not an Illness".(Old Tappen, N. J.: Fleming H. Revell company, 1980), p. 71.

7. Robert B. McCready, "Our Bed is Flourishing." (New York: Sheed and Ward, 1969), p.17

8. Ibid, p.18.

9. Ibid, p.18.

10. Jay E. Adams, "Pastoral counseling." (Grand Rapids: Baker Book House, 1977), p. 77.

11. Ibid

12. James Pike, "If You Marry Outside Your Faith". (New York: Harper and Rowe, Inc., 1954), p. 23.

13. Ibid

14. Ibid, p.24.

15. Ibid, p. 25

16. Narramore, p.89

17. Ibid

18. Ibid, p. 31

19. Col. 3:20-21

Chapter three

1. W. L. Herbert and F. V. Jarvis, "The Art of Marriage Counseling." (New York: Emerson Books, Inc, 1960), p. 36

2. Ibid

3. Eph. 5:25

4. Norman H. Wright, "Marital counseling." (Denver: Christian Marriage Enrichment, 1981), p.11

5. Ibid, p.5

6. Ibid

7. Ibid

8. Robert B. McCready, "Our Bed is Flourishing." (New York: Sheed and Ward, 1969), p.63.

9. Ibid

10. W. L. Herbert, et al., p.36

11. Wright, p. 91

12. McCready, p.148.

13. Ibid

Chapter four

1.   W. L. Herbert and F. V. Jarvis, "The Art of Marital counseling." (New York : Emerson Books, Inc., 1960), p. 36.

2.   Ibid, p.40.

3.   Ibid

4.   Prov. 22:6

5.   David A. Schulz and Stanley F. Rogers, "Marriage, The Family, and Personal Fulfillment." (Englewood Cliffs, N. J. Prentice Hall, Inc, 1975), p. 45.

6.   Charles E. Rosenberg, "The Family in History." (Pittsburgh: University of Pennsylvania Press, 1975), p.179.

7.   Douglas W. Cole, "When Families hurt". (Nashville: Broadman Press, 1979), p. 46

8.   Ibid

9.   Ibid

10. Ibid

Chapter five

1. Elizabeth R. Skoglund, "To Anger with Love." (New York: Harper and Rowe.1977), p. 10

2. Jay E. Adams, "More Than Redemption." (Grand Rapids: Baker Book House, 1979), p. 277

3. Ibid

4. Ibid

5. Stanley E. Anderson P, "Every Pastor a Counselor." (Wheaton, Ill.: Van Kampen Press, 1949), p.36

6. Ibid, p.49.

7. Ibid, p.56.

8. James Dobson, "Emotions: Can you trust them."(Minneapolis: World-wide, 1980), p.85.

9. Ibid

10. David W. Augsburger, "Anger and Assertiveness in Pastoral Care." (Philadelphia: Fortress Press, 1979), p.25.

11. Ibid

Chapter six

1. Robert B. McCready, "Our Bed is flourishing." (New York Sheed and Ward, 1969), p.30.

2. Roger W. Smith," Guilt and Society." New York: Anchor Books, Doubleday and Company, Inc, 1971), p. 135.

3. Ibid, p.136.

4. Nathan S. Kline, "From Sad to Glad." (New York: Ballentine Books, 1979), p.1

5. Don Baker and Emery Nester, "Depression." (Portland: Multnomah Press, 1983), p. 31.

6. Ibid

7. Kline, p. 1

8. Ibid, p.2.

9. Ibid

10. Ibid

11. Ibid

12. Jay E. Adams, "The Big Umbrella." (Nutley, N. J. Presbyterian and Reformed Press, 1973), p. 43.

13. Christina Baldwin, "One to One." (New York, M. Evans and Company, 1977), p. 27

14. Howard J. Clinebell, "The Mental Health Ministry of the Local Church." (Nashville: Abingdon, 1972), p.13.

15. Ibid

16. Ibid

17. John, 8:5-11.

18. Paul B. Maves, "The Church and Mental Health". New York; Charles Scribner and Sons, 1953), p. 43,44.

19. Ibid

Chapter seven

1. Nathan S. Kline, "From Sad to Glad." (New York: Ballentine Books, 1971), p. 1.

2. Eugene Kennedy," Crisis counseling." (New York: Continuum,1981), p. 43.

3. Howard J Clinebell, "Basic Types of Pastoral Counseling." (Nashville: Abingdon Press, 1966), p. 6.

4. Ibid, p.158.

5. Isiah 9:6

6. Proverbs 11:14

7. Romans12:2

8. Clinebell, p. 60

9. William E. Crane, "Where God Comes In." (Waco, Texas: Word Books, Publishers, 1970), p. 67.

10. Jay E. Adams, "Coping With Counseling Crisis." (Grand Rapids : Baker Book House, 1976), p. 9.

11. Ibid, p. 23

12. Kennedy, p. 47

13. Diana Sullivan Everstine and Louis Everstine, "People in Crisis." (New York: Bruner, Mazel, Publishers, 1983), p. 201.

14. Bruce S Narramore, "No Condemnation." (Grand Rapids: Academic Books, Zondervan Publishing House, 1984), p. 16

Chapter eight

1. Elizabeth Kubler-Ross, "On Death and Dying." (New York: Macmillan Publishing Co., 1969), p. 38

2. Ira J. Tanner, "The Gift of Grief." (New York: Hawthorn Books, 1976), p. 143

3. Richard N. Soulten, "Care For the Dying." (Atlanta: John Knox Press, 1978) p. 49

4. Psalms 39: 12—13.

5. Jay E. Adams, "The Big Umbrella." (Nutley, N J: Presbyterian and Reformed Publishing Co., 1973), p.5

6. Ibid, p. 4

7. Ibid

8. Ibid, p. 65

9. Tanner, p. 7

10. Ibid

11. Ibid, p. 2

12. Ibid

13. Ibid, p. 143

14. Ibid, p. 144

15. Ibid

Bibliography

Adams, Jay E. "Coping with Counseling Crisis." Grand Rapids: Baker Book House, 1976.

Adams, Jay E. "Matters of Concern to Christian Counselors." Baker Book House, 1979.

Adams, Jay E. "More Than Redemption." Baker Book House, 1979.

Adams, Jay E. "Pastoral Counseling." Baker Book, House, 1977.

Adams, Jay E. "The Big Umbrella." Nutley, N J: Presbyterian Reformed Publishing Co., 1973.

Anderson, Stanley E. "Every Pastor a Counselor." Wheaton, Ill.: Van Kampen Press, 1952.

Anderson, Terrence R. et al "Care For the Dying." Atlanta: John Knox Press, 1978.

Augsburger, David W. "Anger and Assertiveness in Pastoral Care." Philadelphia: Fortress, Press, 1979.

Baker, Don, and Emery Nester. "Depression." Portland: Multnomah Press, 1983.

Baldwin, Christina. "One to One." New York: M. Evans and Company, 1977.

Clinebell, Howard J. "Basic Types of Pastoral Counseling." Nashville: Abingdon Press, 1967.

Clinebell, Howard J. "The Mental Health Ministry of The Local Church." Nashville: Abingdon Press, 1972.

Cole, W. D. "When Families hurt." Nashville: Broadman Press, 1979.

Crane, William E. "Where God Comes In." Waco Texas: World Books, 1970.

Dobson, James. "Emotions: Can You trust them?" Minneapolis: World Wide, 1980.

Dobson, James. "Emotions, Can You Trust them?" New York; Bantam Books, 1982.

Everstine, Diana Sullivan, and Louis Everstine. "People in Crisis." New York: Brenner, Mazel, Publishers, 1983.

Frankl, Victor E. "The Will to Meaning." New York: New American Library, 1970.

Herbert, W. L. and F. V. Jarvis, "The Art of Marriage counseling." New York: Emerson Books, 1960.

Hesselgrave, David J. "Counseling Cross-Culturally." Grand Rapids: Baker Book House, 1984.

Ishee, John. "When trouble comes." Nashville: Broadman Press, 1970.

James, Muriel M. "Born to Love." New York: Bantam Books, 1970.

Kennedy, Eugene. "Crisis Counseling." New York: Continuum press, 1981.

Kline, Nathan, S. "From Sad to Glad." New York: Ballentine Books, 1971.

Kubler-Ross, Elisabeth "On Death and Dying." New York: Macmillan Publishing Co. 1970.

Maves, Paul B. "The Church and Mental Health." New York: Charles Scribner and Sons, 1952.

McCready, Robert B. "Our Bed is Flourishing." New York: Sheed and Ward, 1969.

Narramore, Bruce. "Adolescence is not an Illness." Old Tappan, N. J: Fleming H. Revell Co., 1980.

Narramore, Bruce. "No Condemnation." Grand Rapids: Academic Books, 1984.

Pike, James A. "If You Marry Outside Your Faith." New York: Harper and Rowe, 1959.

Rosenberg, Charles E. "The Family in History." Pittsburgh: University of Penn. Press, 1975.

Schulz, David A. and Stanley F. Rodgers. "Marriage, The Family and Personal Fulfillment." Englewood Cliffs, N. J.: Prentice Hall. Inc., 1975.

Skoglund, Elizabeth R. "To Anger With Love." New York: Harper and Rowe, 1977.

Smith, Roger W "Guilt: Man and Society." New York: Anchor Books, Doubleday and Co. Inc., 1971.

Tanner, Ira J. "The Gift of Grief." New York: Continuum press, 1981.

Underwood, Ralph L. "Empathy and Confrontation in Pastoral Care." Philadelphia: Fortress Press, 1985.

Wright, H Norman. "Marital Counseling." Denver: Christian Marriage Enrichment, 1981.

Glossary of Terms

1. Adolescence, The period of physical and Psychological development from onset of puberty to maturity.

2. Apathetic, Feeling or displaying little or no emotion.

3. Aptitude, A natural or acquired talent or ability.

4. Cross-cultural, comparing or treating two or more different cultures.

5. Cross-cultural Counseling, A counselor trained to counsel clients or patients from a different culture, race, or ethnic background than his or her own.

6. Christian, Declaring belief in Jesus Christ as Savior.

7. Complex, Modern society with mass automation, the computer age, involved or complicated.

8. Comprehend, To understand, to grasp mentally.

9. Conflict, A state of being torn between competing forces.

10. Contemporaries, About the same age, belonging to the same period of time.

11. Delinquent, Failing to do required duty, or what is required by law. (Example, Juvenile delinquent).

12. Depression, Melancholy, sadness, feelings of dejection.

13. Deviant behavior, A departure from normal behavior, unlawful behavior.

14. Dimension, Scope or magnitude.

15. Disillusioned, To disappoint, or make bitter.

16. Edify, To enlighten or instruct, to encourage, to foster intellectual, moral, or spiritual development.

17. Environment, The circumstances or conditions surrounding a person, in which one lives.

18. External locus of control, Externally directed, a person who has not developed an adequate sense of inner direction but has to be controlled by being told what to do. One who does not respect rules, mores etc. of society.

19. Internal locus of control, One who has internalized the rules, customs, mores of society by abiding by them while maturing from a child to adulthood thereby becoming inner directed,

20. Formative (years), Years of growth and development.

21. Germaine, Relevant to a point.

22. Hierarchy (family), Order or rank from oldest to youngest by age.

23. Holy Spirit, Third Person of the Christian Trinity.

24. Hospice, An establishment or program caring for the physical, emotional, and spiritual needs of the terminally ill patient.

25. Idiosyncratic, Temperament or mental constitution peculiar to a person or group, mannerisms etc.

26. Immortal, Living or lasting forever.

27. Indigenous, Native, occurring naturally in a specific area or group.

28. Integrated, To bring together into a whole.

29. Intercession, To intervene or intercede, or petition on another's behalf.

30. Linear, Of or relating to a line or lines.

31. Malady, Disease, disorder, or ailment.

32. Mediate, To settle or resolve differences.

33. Milieu, Environment.

34. Methodologies, The system of principles, procedures, and practices applied to a particular branch of knowledge.

35. Neurotic (neurosis), One of a large group of non-psychotic disorders characterized by unrealistic anxiety and other associated problems. For example: phobic avoidances, obsessions, and compulsions.

36. Permeable, Open to passage or penetration.

37. Philosophy of life, Selecting your guiding principles, your life goals.

38. Propitiation, Win or regain the good will of. Sacrifices made to regain favor or good will. For example: Jesus was the propitiation for our sins, (satisfaction to God).

39. Psychosomatic, A physical disorder in the body, originating in or aggravated by the psychic or emotional process of an individual.

40. Psychosocial, Of or pertaining to the psychological development of the individual in relation to his social environment.

41. Psychotherapy, Treatment of a mental disorder by various means involving communication between a trained person and the patient including suggestion, counseling, and psychoanalysis.

42. Psychotic, A severe mental disorder in which thinking and emotion are so impaired that the individual is seriously out of contact with reality.

43. Reaction Formation, A defense mechanism whereby an unconscious and unacceptable impulse or feeling which would cause anxiety is converted into its opposite so that it can become conscious and be expressed.

44. Remnant, What is left over, remainder, residue, a small remaining part.

45. Sabotage, A deliberate action aimed at weakening an enemy, person, or thing through subversion, disruption, or terrorism.

46. Secular, Worldly rather than Spiritual.

47. Somatic, Of the body as distinguished from the soul, mind, or psyche, physical.

48. Soul, An entity regarded as being the immortal or Spiritual part of the person. The moral or emotional nature of man.

49. Sphere, Field of knowledge, or activity.

50. Stigma, Something that detracts from the character of a person or reputation of a person or group.

51. Truant, Pupil or student who stays away from or skips school.

52. Truant Officer, An officer who locates and returns truant students to school.

53. Usurp, To hold property, position, or power without right.

54. Validation, To declare valid, to prove to be valid, to give legal force to.

References for glossary of terms are as follows: Davison, Gerald C., and Neal, John M. Abnormal Psychology. New York: John Wiley and sons, Inc., 1982, definitions for words numbered: 34, 42, and 43.

Guralnik, David B: Webster's New World Dictionary. Englewood Cliffs, N. J: Prentice Hall, Inc., 1972, defined all other words in the glossary except the ones listed below and above.

Words cited in the glossary were defined by the writer: # 5, 7, 18, 19 and 52.

978-0-595-40101-7
0-595-40101-5

Printed in the United States
83807LV00005B/1-30/A